Tolley's Company Secretary's Checklists

by Matthew Baker FCIS, MBA

Cobbetts, Solicitors

Members of the LexisNexis Group worldwide

United Kingdom	LexisNexis Butterworths Tolley, a Division of Reed Elsevier (UK) Ltd, 2 Addiscombe Road, CROYDON CR9 5AF
Argentina	LexisNexis Argentina, BUENOS AIRES
Australia	LexisNexis Butterworths, CHATSWOOD, New South Wales
Austria	LexisNexis Verlag ARD Orac GmbH & Co KG, VIENNA
Canada	LexisNexis Butterworths Canada Ltd, MARKHAM, Ontario
Chile	LexisNexis Chile Ltda, SANTIAGO DE CHILE
Czech Republic	Nakladatelství Orac sro, PRAGUE
France	Editions du Juris-Classeur SA, PARIS
Hong Kong	LexisNexis Butterworths, HONG KONG
Hungary	Hvg Orac, BUDAPEST
India	LexisNexis Butterworths, NEW DELHI
Ireland	Butterworths (Ireland) Ltd, DUBLIN
Italy	Giuffré Editore, MILAN
Malaysia	Malayan Law Journal Sdn Bhd, KUALA LUMPUR
New Zealand	LexisNexis Butterworths, WELLINGTON
Poland	Wydawnictwo Prawnicze LexisNexis, WARSAW
Singapore	LexisNexis Butterworths, SINGAPORE
South Africa	LexisNexis Butterworths, DURBAN
Switzerland	Stämpfli Verlag AG, BERNE
USA	LexisNexis, DAYTON, Ohio

ISBN 0 7545 1897 3

Typeset by Letterpart Ltd, Reigate, Surrey.

Printed and bound in Great Britain by The Cromwell Press Limited, Trowbridge, Wiltshire.

Visit Butterworths LexisNexis *direct* at www.butterworths.com

Preface

For a number of years I have produced checklists for company secretaries in respect of the accounts of listed companies. These checklists cover, for instance, corporate governance disclosures, notice of general meeting and the remuneration report. Roger Thomas and Julie Clarke of LexisNexis Butterworths Tolley asked if this could be expanded to make a book of checklists as a companion to their Company Secretarial Handbook.

This is the resulting book which has been compiled to provide a brief guidance on legal and company secretarial requirements for various actions a company may take. They omit, for example, certain matters that would normally be outside the remit of the company secretary. Throughout I have attempted to focus on the matters a company secretary practically needs to be aware of. The Checklists are therefore not designed to give a complete coverage of the subject referred to but rather are intended as a guide of issues to consider.

The Checklists encompass a range of activities from the technically difficult to the more straightforward and I have attempted to treat these in a consistent manner. Also I am conscious that those referring to the checklists will range from experts in their field to the newly-qualified or occasional user, and therefore I have tried to steer away from jargon where possible.

I have, as appropriate, highlighted some of the proposals pursuant to the final report of the Company Law Review Steering Group. In addition, the new disclosure requirements on the remuneration of directors of listed companies are covered; many thanks to Hugh Simpson for these.

Finally I would like to thank Victoria Willcox and Laura Forbes, both of the company secretarial team at Cobbetts, and Debra Somekh, Shirley Gitlin, Emma Davies and Vikki Launders of Addleshaw Booth & Co.

November 2002
Matthew Baker FCIS, MBA
Cobbetts, Solicitors

Contents

1 The Company Secretary

Contents

1.1 Appointment of Secretary

Section 283 of the *Companies Act 1985* (*CA 1985*) requires that each company must have a secretary. In July 2001, the Department of Trade and Industry issued the Final Report of the Company Law Review Steering Group which suggested that private limited companies will not be required to have a secretary.

Notwithstanding this, the secretary is an essential officer in the day-to-day running of a company (see Checklist 1.3).

Companies House Form 10, filed by a company on incorporation, provides for the appointment of the first secretary of the company. This checklist concentrates on the procedure thereafter. Such a procedure is defined by a company's Articles (see Checklist 2.3).

Company Secretary's Handbook reference: CSH 1.9.

When proposing to appoint a company secretary, the following should be considered.

	Task:	**Reference:**	
1.	Is the person an undischarged bankrupt, suffering from a mental disorder, or a disqualified director?		☐
2.	Has the appointment been approved by the board of directors?	**Checklist 6.3**	☐
3.	For public companies, is the person appointed secretary appropriately qualified, for example, a member of the Institute of Chartered Secretaries and Administrators or one of the Chartered Accounting bodies?	***CA 1985, s 286***	☐
4.	Has the individual consented to act as secretary, by the signing of Form 288a?		☐
5.	Has Form 288a been submitted to Companies House within 14 days of the date of appointment?	***CA 1985, s 288(2)*** **Checklist 5.1**	☐
6.	Has the register of secretaries been updated to reflect the appointment of a new secretary?	***CA 1985, s 288(1)*** **Checklist 3.2**	☐
7.	Does the company's bank mandate need to be changed?		☐
8.	Does the company's directors and officers indemnity insurance need to be altered?		☐

Practical Notes

The Articles of Association of most companies make the appointment of the secretary a matter for the directors (CA 1985, Table A, Reg 99).

Listed companies should also notify their regulatory authority and the exchange on which the shares are listed as the secretary will usually be their main point of contact. Furthermore, it is possible that the Listing Rules of the relevant exchange will require that an announcement is made regarding the change of secretary.

Companies may appoint a deputy secretary to deputise for the secretary in their absence. If the Articles of Association of the company allow, a joint or second secretary with equal authority may also be appointed.

1.2   Resignation and Removal of the Secretary

Companies House Form 10 filed on incorporation provides for the appointment of the first secretary of the company. This checklist concentrates on the procedure thereafter. Such a procedure is defined by a company's Articles (see Checklist 2.3).

Company Secretary's Handbook reference: CSH 1.10

When a company secretary has resigned or you are proposing to remove the current secretary, the following should be considered.

Task:	Reference:	✍
1. Has the individual resigned as the secretary and do you have a letter of resignation?		☐
2. If the individual has not resigned, has the board approved the removal of the secretary or followed such other procedure for the secretary's removal as the Articles may provide?	**Checklist 2.3**	☐
3. Has Form 288b been submitted to Companies House within 14 days of the change of secretary?	*CA 1985, s 288(2)* **Checklist 5.1**	☐
4. Has the register of secretaries been updated to reflect the resignation or removal of the secretary?	*CA 1985, s 288(1)* **Checklist 3.2**	☐
5. Does the company's bank mandate need to be changed?		☐
6. Does the company's directors and officers indemnity insurance need to be altered?		☐
7. Has a new secretary been appointed?	**Checklist 1.1**	☐

Practical Notes

Most Articles of Association make the appointment or removal of the secretary a matter for the directors (CA 1985, Table A, Reg 99).

The Combined Code, which is best practice for companies, states that 'Any question of the removal of the company secretary should be a matter for the board as a whole' (CC A.1.4).

Depending on the nature of the secretary's responsibilities, certain individuals may need to be informed, for example, the professional advisors of the company.

Listed companies should also notify their regulatory authority and the exchange on which the shares are listed as the secretary will usually be their main point of contact. Furthermore, it is possible that the Listing Rules of the relevant exchange will require that an announcement is made regarding the change of secretary.

1.3 Duties of the Company Secretary

Every company must appoint a company secretary to whom the board of directors may delegate the responsibility for compliance with the *Companies Act 1985*, in order that neither the company nor the individual directors become liable for any breaches in compliance. *CA 1985, Sch 24* lists the various statutory penalties that may be imposed following any such breach, which range from a fine to potential imprisonment.

Whilst the remit of the company secretary may vary to some degree from company to company, there are certain specific duties which are typically the responsibility of the company secretary. It is, however, worth highlighting those areas for which the company secretary is liable to have specific responsibility.

When appointing a company secretary, the following should be considered.

Task:	Reference:	✍
1. Have the directors satisfied themselves that the company secretary to be appointed has the necessary qualifications and experience to fulfil this role, noting specific requirements for a public company?	*CA 1985, s 286* **Checklist 2.11**	☐
2. Is the company secretary ensuring that:		
2.1 the statutory registers are up to date;	**Checklists 3.1–3.5**	☐
2.2 board and board committee minutes are maintained in an appropriate minute book;	**Checklist 3.6**	☐
2.3 board and general meetings are held in a timely and appropriate manner;	**Checklist 6.3**	☐
2.4 minutes of general meetings are maintained in an appropriate minute book;	**Checklist 3.6**	☐
2.5 statutory returns and resolutions, such as the annual return, are filed as required and in a timely manner;	**Checklist 5.1**	☐
2.6 the annual accounts are completed, filed and circulated to shareholders in a timely manner;	**Checklists 7.1–7.11**	☐
2.7 the company is ensuring compliance with other Regulations, for example the Listing Rules; and	**Checklist 3.9**	☐
2.8 documentation is maintained, for instance, Memorandum and Articles of Association and directors' service contracts?	**Checklists 2.1 and 2.3**	☐

Practical Notes

The intention in these checklists is to focus on the company secretary's duties and to provide guidance to assist us overcoming some of the many pitfalls and ensure compliance with the requirements of the Companies Act 1985.

The company secretary is an 'officer' of the company (CA 1985, s 744). Thus the company secretary as well as the directors can also be liable for any breaches of the Companies Act 1985.

2 The Company Constitution

Contents

2.1 Memorandum of Association

Two or more persons who are associated for a lawful purpose may subscribe to the Memorandum of Association in order to form a limited or an unlimited company (*CA 1985, s 1*).

The Memorandum sets out essential information on the company such as its name, the type of company, objectives and the extent of the liability of the members. The objects of the company are dealt with separately (see Checklist 2.2)

Company Secretary's Handbook reference: Appendix 2C.

Does the Memorandum of Association of a limited company include the following?

Task:		Reference:	✎
1.	The name of the company?	*CA 1985, s 2(1)(a)* **Checklist 2.8** **CSH 2.20**	☐
2.	In the case of a public company, that the company is a public limited company?	*CA 1985, s 25* **CSH 2.31**	☐
3.	Whether the company is domiciled in England and Wales, or Scotland?	*CA 1985, s 2(b)*	☐
4.	The objects of the company including, for example, the ability to borrow and enter into guarantees, take directors' and officers' liability insurance and, for a private company, in respect of financial assistance?	*CA 1985, s 2(1)(c)* **Checklist 2.2**	☐
5.	The amount of the share capital with which the company proposes to be registered or was registered and how that capital is divided (unless it is an unlimited company or a company limited by guarantee)?	*CA 1985, s 2(5)* **Checklist 8.1**	☐
6.	In the case of a guarantee company, does it state the amount each member undertakes to contribute to the assets of the company in the event of it being wound up?	**CSH 2.28**	☐
7.	The names of the subscribers, and in the case of a company limited by shares, the number of shares to be taken by each?	*CA 1985, s 2(5)(c)* **CSH 2.32**	☐

Practical Notes

The basic formats for Memorandum are set out in the Companies (Tables A to F) Regulations 1985 (SI 1985/805).

- *Table B in the case of a private company limited by shares;*
- *Table C in the case of a company limited by guarantee;*
- *Table E in the case of an unlimited company; and*
- *Table F in the case of a public limited company.*

A company may include additional provisions in its Memorandum of Association that are not required by the Companies Act 1985.

On incorporation, the Memorandum must be signed by each subscriber. The subscribers are the initial members who should be entered in the register of members (see Checklist 3.1) on incorporation (see Checklist 2.4).

If provisions in the Articles of Association conflict with the Companies Act 1985, these provisions will not be effective (CA 1985, s 14). Similarly if provisions in the Articles conflict with the Memorandum of Association, the latter takes precedence.

A special resolution is required to amend the objects of the Memorandum of Association (Checklist 7.1), (CA 1985, s 4). A company may also pass a resolution to change the company name (Checklist 2.8). Where alterations are made to the Memorandum every copy of the Memorandum issued after the alteration has been made must include the alteration (CA 1985, s 20).

2.2   Objects of the Company

In the UK, the objects of a company usually comprise the largest part of the Memorandum of Association (see Checklist 2.1). The objects set out the purpose for which the company exists. There is no prescribed form for the objects of a company however the following questions should be considered.

Task:	Reference:	✍
1. Does it contain the main business and activities of the company?	**CSH 2.24**	☐
2. Are there ancillary clauses allowing the company to achieve its main object stated, for example power to:	**CSH 2.24**	☐
2.1 borrow and lend money;		☐
2.2 purchase and sell property;		☐
2.3 acquire and promote other businesses;		☐
2.4 act as the attorney; or	**Checklist 8.10**	☐
2.5 give guarantees.		☐
3. Does it include 'catch all' clauses to allow a company to do anything incidental to the main objects, including a general commercial objective as defined by *CA 1985, s 3A*?	*CA 1985, s 3A* **CSH 2.24-2.26**	☐

Practical Notes

Although CA 1985, s 35A(1) and s 108 virtually abolished the concept of 'ultra vires', where a company operates outside the objectives, as regard third parties, the directors could be personally liable to account to the company's shareholders in circumstances where they have exceeded the powers given to them in the Memorandum of Association to bind the company (CA 1985, s 35).

The concept of ultra vires had far greater importance historically. The vast majority of companies currently have widely-drawn objects which impose few restrictions. However, as banks are generally extremely cautious when checking the Memorandum, an appropriate amount of emphasis needs to be given to the ability of the company to lend and borrow money and to enter into guarantees.

It is generally good to have a descriptive first clause to the objects so as to allow third parties to judge the nature of the business.

Charities and companies limited by guarantee often have more restrictive and precise Memorandum and Articles of Association, which – in the case of charities – restrict the actions of the company to purely charitable actions and restrict the distribution of monies to organisations with similar objects.

A special resolution is required to amend the objects of the Memorandum of Association (see Checklist 7.1) (CA 1985, s 4). Where alterations are made to a company's Memorandum, every copy of the Memorandum issued after the alteration has been made must include the alteration (CA 1985, s 20).

2.3   Articles of Association

The Memorandum and Articles of Association are a contract, the effect of which is to create obligations binding on the members in their dealings with the company, and on the company in its dealings with the member.

The Articles of Association set out a company's regulations for its internal management. *Table A* of the *Companies Act 1985* sets out a model set of Articles for a company limited by shares. It applies to both public and private limited companies which are limited by shares and with certain modifications introduced by *Table C* and *Table E* to private limited companies limited by guarantee and unlimited companies respectively. If, for instance, a company limited by shares has not registered any Articles, *Table A* applies. Even if a company limited by shares registers its own Articles, *Table A* will apply as far as the Articles do not conflict with *Table A*.

Company Secretary's Handbook reference: CSH 2.34–2.39

When looking at the Articles of Association, the following should be considered:

Task:	**Reference:**	✍
1. Is there anything in the Articles that conflicts with statutory requirements?	*CA 1985, s 14*	☐
2. Is there anything in the Articles that conflicts with the Memorandum, as the Memorandum takes precedence?	**Checklist 2.1**	☐
3. To which version of statutory tables do the Articles refer, if any?	*CA 1985, Table A*	☐
4. Are the regulations divided into paragraphs and numbered consecutively?	*CA 1985, s 7(3)*	☐
5. When asked to review Articles, the following are some of the areas on which to focus.		☐
5.1 In terms of share capital, are there any restrictions varying, for example, from class rights or rights to dividends and voting?	**Checklist 8.1** **Checklist 8.4** **Checklist 8.5** **Checklist 8.17**	☐
5.2 Allotments including pre-emption rights and directors authority to issue shares	*CA 1985, ss 80, 95, 189* **Checklist 8.11**	☐
5.3 Transfer of shares, including restrictions such as the pre-emption rights of existing shareholders or requirements for authorisation.	**Checklist 8.13**	☐
5.4 Meetings of directors and shareholders, such as the number required for a quorum, and voting rights.	**Checklist 6.3**	☐
5.5 Appointments and removal of directors which may relate to the rights of the shareholders.	**Checklist 6.1** **Checklist 6.4**	☐
5.6 Whether directors are required to retire by rotation.	**Checklist 7.5**	☐
5.7 Details of any limits on the power of the directors in the future.		☐

Practical Notes

The Articles need to reflect the situation of the company. It is useful to ensure that practical clauses are in place, for example, that directors are able to conduct meetings by telephone.

If the company is a wholly owned subsidiary of another company, it is useful if there is a specific clause in the Articles of the subsidiary company allowing for the appointment and removal of directors by the parent without recourse to s 303 of the Companies Act 1985 (see Checklist 6.4)

Joint venture companies often have complex Articles as they anticipate the future and in this case it is hard to generalise as the Articles should reflect the contribution of each party to the company. It would not be unusual to see complex mechanisms relating to value on a transfer of shares which ensure a level of protection to the minority shareholders.

If the Articles of Association refer to another document, that document forms part of the Articles of Association and needs to be placed on the public record by filing it at Companies House (see Checklist 5.1).

Subject to the provisions of the Companies Act 1985 and to the provisions contained in the Memorandum (see Checklist 2.1) a company may alter its Articles by special resolution (CA 1985, s 9) (see Checklist 7.1).

2.4   Incorporation

Incorporation is the term used to describe the creation of corporate entities. Many companies are bought 'ready-made' as shelf companies and then transferred to a new owner. However, the procedure to create a company is straightforward and should be given consideration (unless time is a constraint).

Companies can be incorporated electronically using a slightly different procedure but this is not described here.

Company Secretary's Handbook reference: Appendix 2A

When proposing to incorporate a company, the following should be considered.

Task:		Reference:	✍
1.	Has tax advice been taken as to whether you will be best trading as a company rather than as an individual?	**CSH 2.2**	☐
2.	Is the proposed company name available?	*CA 1985, s 28* **Checklist 2.8** **CSH 2.9-2.10**	☐
3.	Have you gathered the names and addresses of the proposed shareholders and secretary?		☐
4.	Have you received details of the individual/organisations to whom the subscriber share is to be transferred (if any)?		☐
5.	Do you know how many shares and the type of shares (if other than ordinary) each proposed shareholder intends to take initially?		☐
6.	For the proposed directors, have you collected the names, addresses, dates of birth, occupations, former names, nationalities and additionally any UK directorships they have held in the last five years?		☐
7.	Are the Articles appropriately worded to regulate the relationship between the shareholders and to define how the company will be run?	**Checklist 2.3** **CSH 2.34-2.39**	☐
8.	Have your prepared the Memorandum of Association to set out the objects of the company and do they include, for example, the correct name of the company	*CA 1985, s 2* **Checklist 2.1** **CSH 2.20-2.33**	☐
9.	Have you ensured that the following have been completed properly and executed by the appropriate parties?	*CA 1985, s 10*	☐
	9.1 Memorandum of Association (signed and witnessed by the subscribers, indicating their names and addresses and the number of shares each subscriber is taking on incorporation).		☐
	9.2 Articles of Association (signed and witnessed by the subscribers and indicating their name and address).		☐
	9.3 Form 10 providing details of the registered office (within the country of domicile stated in the Memorandum of		☐

        Association and the first officers) signed by both the
        proposed director(s) and secretary and either all the
        shareholders, or an agent on behalf of all the shareholders?

10. Have you checked that the documents referred to in point 9 above   ***CA 1985, s 12***   ☐
      are all properly completed and dated? If so, complete Form 12
      (declaration that the incorporation documents are in order;
      solicitors or Commissioner for Oaths should charge £5 for the
      declaring of each Form 10).

11. Have all the items listed in points 8 and 9 above been filed at   **Checklist 5.1**   ☐
      Companies House together with a cheque for the sum of £20 (fee
      correct at the time of writing)?

12. Have you received the certificate of incorporation which is   ***CA 1985, s 13(7)***   ☐
      conclusive proof of the incorporation of the company?   **CSH 2.49**

Practical Notes

A company limited by shares need not submit Articles of Association with its application for incorporation but may rely on Table A. However, the vast majority of companies register Articles of Association more tailored to the intended purpose for the company (see Checklist 2.3).

There is a same day incorporation service for which Companies House, at the time of writing, charges £80. The standard service takes seven to ten working days.

Most companies are incorporated with standard form Memorandum and Articles of Association which are available from stationery suppliers. It is worth investing time during the initial stage to ensure these documents (which form the basis of the company) are in the most appropriate form.

If an error is made in the initial documentation such that Companies House rejects it, then Form 12 needs to be completed and submitted again. The most common error is a failure to ensure that the forms and Memorandum and Articles of Association have been executed properly.

Where time is of the essence, a 'ready-made' company should be considered. The exact procedure will depend on the company formation agents involved. Typically, the first step is to order a shelf company from a formation agent who have a ready stock of suitable companies and will provide details of its name, number and registered office.

2.5 Limited Liability Partnerships (LLPs)

These are a reasonably new phenomena created by the *Limited Liability Partnerships Act 2000*. The new entity functions as a partnership but with limited liability for its members. However a member's personal assets may still be at risk, for example in a claim of negligence.

The intention was that LLPs would be used as a vehicle for professional practices and a number of partnerships have converted. However, at the time of writing, the requirements to make a public financial disclosure have dissuaded larger numbers from making this change.

When proposing to incorporate a limited liability partnership, the following are questions to consider.

Task:	Reference:	✍
1. Is the name available and does it end in the words 'limited liability partnership'?	**Checklist 2.8**	☐
2. Has a Form LLP2 been completed which includes the following:	***LLPA 2000, s 2(2)(a)-(f)*** **CSH 2.74**	☐
2.1 name of the entity;		☐
2.2 situation and address of the registered office;		☐
2.3 full names and addresses of the persons who are to be members on incorporation; and		☐
2.4 details of the designated members?	***LLPA 2000, s 2(1)(c)***	☐
3. Has the statement of compliance on Form LLP2 been signed by a solicitor or proposed member indicating in what capacity they are signing?		☐
4. Have all the members or designated members signed and dated the incorporation document to confirm their consent to act?		☐
5. Has a partnership agreement been prepared, if necessary?	***LLPA 2000, s 5(1)(a)*** **CSH 2.77**	☐
6. Do you have the remittance fee of £95 (at the time of publication)?		☐
7. Have you filed all the necessary documents at Companies House?	**Checklist 5.1**	☐
8. Have you received the certificate of incorporation?		☐

Practical Notes

The LLP is required to have at least two designated members at all times. The designated members carry out similar duties to those of the directors and secretary (CSH 2.76).

2.6   Post-incorporation Considerations

Having incorporated the company there are a variety of matters to consider to ensure that the company is adapted to the future needs of the business. It is worth taking time at this stage to ensure that everything is in order rather than having to correct something at a later date.

Company Secretary's Handbook reference: CSH 2.85

When dealing with post-incorporation matters, the following should be taken into consideration.

Task:	Reference:	✍
1. Have you elected a Chairman, if appropriate?		☐
2. Are you intending to appoint further directors?	**Checklist 6.1**	☐
3. Is the company going to adopt a company seal (this is not essential)?		☐
4. Is the intention to leave the registered office of the company at its current location?	**Checklist 3.7**	☐
5. Is the preferred accounting reference date in place?	**Checklist 4.1**	☐
6. Have auditors been appointed, if necessary?	**Checklist 4.17**	☐
7. Have bankers for the company been appointed and a bank account opened?		☐
8. Do the statutory registers reflect the position of the company following incorporation?	**Checklists 3.1-3.5**	☐
9. Have any arrangements in respect of obtaining further capital and relating to possible alterations in share capital been discussed?	**Checklist 8.1** **Checklist 8.11**	☐
10. Have any pre-incorporation contracts made by the promoters been adopted and the directors service contacts considered?	*CA 1985, s 36C*	☐
11. Have the directors notified the company of any interest they have in the company shares pursuant to the *s 324, CA 1985*, and interests contracts pursuant to *s 317, CA 1985*?	**Checklist 6.6**	☐
12. Does the company need to register for Value Added Tax and if yes has it done so?		☐
13. Does the company need to apply for the registration of any trade and service marks discussed?		☐
14. Is the company stationary in order?	**Checklist 3.10**	☐
15. If the company is a private company, will it wish to hold annual meetings of the members and if not has the company adopted the elective regime?	**Checklist 7.7**	☐

16. Is it proposed to issue further shares?   **Checklist 8.11**   ☐

17. Do any share certificates need issuing?   *CA 1985, s 185*   ☐
                                                                     Checklist 8.15

18. Are all the statutory registers to be kept at the registered office of   **Checklist 3.11**   ☐
     the company and if not have appropriate notifications been made?

19. Are the Articles of Association appropriate for the current   **Checklist 2.3**   ☐
     circumstances of the company?

20. Is appropriate insurance in place e.g. in respect of any properties   ☐
     the company owns?

Practical Notes

Companies are incorporated for a variety of purposes and the above is therefore only a list of suggestions. In addition, the specific circumstances of the company will probably necessitate further action.

2.7   Dissolution

Companies usually cease to exist when they are dissolved or 'struck off' the register. A company may initiate the dissolution or it may be imposed on the company by its creditors or by the court. Dissolution is an easier and cheaper way of eliminating a company rather than liquidation although it is still a lengthy process.

In this checklist we are looking at the procedure to follow when the company initiates the dissolution.

When proposing to dissolve a company, the following checklist should be considered.

Task:	Reference:	✍
1. Has the company any assets or liabilities (as these should be reduced as far as possible)?	**CSH 9.16**	☐
2. Have you ensured that in the last three months the company has not:	*CA 1985, s 652B(1)* **CSH 9.20**	☐
2.1 changed name;		☐
2.2 traded or otherwise carried on business;		☐
2.3 made a disposal for value of property or rights which, immediately before ceasing to trade or carry on business, it held for the purpose of disposal for gain in the normal course of trading or otherwise carrying on business; and		☐
2.4 engaged in any activity, except one which is:		☐
2.4.1 necessary or expedient for the purpose of making an application under *CA 1985, s 652A* or deciding whether to do so;		☐
2.4.2 necessary or expedient for the purpose of concluding the affairs of the company;		☐
2.4.3 necessary or expedient for the purpose of complying with any statutory requirements; or		☐
2.4.4 specified by the Secretary of State?		☐
3. Have you ensured that:	*CA 1985, s 652B(3)*	☐
3.1 the company is not subject to an administration order and a receiver of a judicial fact has been appointed;		☐
3.2 an application has been made under *CA 1985, s 425*; and		☐
3.3 a voluntary arrangement in respect of the company has been proposed and made?		☐

4.   Have the majority of the directors completed Form 652a and filed
this at Companies House together with a filing fee of £10 (correct
at time of writing)?

CA 1985, s 652A(2)
Checklist 5.1

☐

5.   Have the following persons been notified within seven days of
the application in writing at the proper address (by post is
acceptable):

CA 1985 ss 652B(6),
652D(1)
CSH 9.22

5.1   all members of the company;   ☐

5.2   all employees of the company;   ☐

5.3   all creditors;   ☐

5.4   any director who has not completed Form 652a; and   ☐

5.5   any manager or trustee of any pension fund established for   ☐
the benefit of the employees of the company?

6.   A month after registration at Companies House, have you   ☐
received a notification that the application has been lodged in the
London Gazette?

7.   Approximately 100 days from the notice of dissolution appearing   ☐
in the London Gazette have you checked with Companies House
to ensure that the company has been dissolved?

Practical Notes

Considerable care needs to be taken prior to the proposed dissolution to ensure that all outstanding matters are finalised. It is important to take time to ensure everything is in order as it is far more difficult to restore a company than it is to dissolve it.

Immediately prior to the dissolution of the company, you should receive notification from Companies House that it will take place a few days hence and that this process is irreversible. Prior to receipt of this notification it is possible to halt the dissolution process (CA 1985, s 652C).

A member or creditor may within 20 years of the publication in the London Gazette of the notice of dissolution of the company can apply for the company to be restored to the register (Checklist 2.13).

If the company has traded in the recent past but has not obtained approval from the Inland Revenue for the dissolution, it is highly likely they will seek to block the dissolution of the company (at least temporarily). Similarly, advice should be sought if items remain on the balance sheet at the time of dissolution (if the company being dissolved is part of a group, it could result in, for example, a tax charge elsewhere in the group).

The liability (if any) of every director and member of the company continues after dissolution for a period of 20 years (CSH 9.26), (see Checklist 2.13).

2.8   Company Names

A change of name may be compulsory if directed by the Registrar of Companies, or more usually voluntary if a company chooses to re-register under a new name.

In principal, a company may choose to register under any name it wishes. Nevertheless, this choice is subject to the rules and restrictions provided by the *ss 25-34* of the *Companies Act 1985*, and the *Business Names Act 1985* (as amended). The objectives of this legislation are to ensure that each company has a distinctive name, and to prevent the registration of names that may be misleading or objectionable.

When applying to change the name of the company the following checklist should be considered.

Task:		Reference:	✍
1.	Unless it is an unlimited company, does the proposed name end with the words 'limited' (for a private company limited by shares or by guarantee), 'public limited company' (for a public limited company), or the appropriate abbreviations or Welsh equivalent?	*CA 1985, ss 25, 27*	☐
2.	Have you checked that the words 'limited', 'unlimited', 'public limited company', their Welsh equivalents or any abbreviations of these words do not appear elsewhere in the proposed name?	*CA 1985, ss 26 (1)(a),(b)*	☐
3.	If the company wishes to omit the use of the word 'limited' (or the appropriate abbreviations or Welsh equivalent) from the end of its name, have the following obligations been satisfied?	*CA 1985, s 30* **CSH 2.15**	☐
3.1	Is the company a private company limited by guarantee or a private company limited by shares which on 25th February 1982 did not include 'limited' in its name owing to a licence granted under *s 19* of the *Companies Act 1948*?		☐
3.2	Are the objects of the company the promotion of either commerce, art, science, education, religion, charity or of any profession?		☐
3.3	Do the Memorandum and Articles of Association of the company state that any profits or other income are applied in promoting the company's objects, the payment of dividends to members of the company is not permitted, and on a winding-up, all the assets of the company will be transferred to another body which has similar objects or of which the objects are the promotion of a charity; and		☐
3.4	Has a statutory declaration in the prescribed form (Form 30(5)(c)) been delivered to the Registrar of Companies to confirm that the Company complies with the above obligations?		☐
4.	Has the Companies House index of companies been checked to confirm that the proposed name is not either the 'same as' or 'too like' an existing name on the register, considering, for example:	*CA 1985, ss 26-28, 714* **CSH 2.10, 2.12**	☐
4.1	that there is a possibility that companies on the register which share the same prefix may be connected (i.e. do they have the same registered office, the same business activity, date of incorporation etc.);		☐

4.2   words such as 'the', 'company', 'and company', cannot be used to differentiate one company from another; and   ☐

4.3   words which are spelt differently but are phonetically identical may not be used?   ☐

5.   Does the proposed name include 'sensitive words' for which the Secretary of State requires justification and if so, have the appropriate approvals been sought?   *CA 1985, ss 26(2)(a),(b)* **CSH 2.11, Appendix 2B See Companies House guidance below**   ☐

6.   Is it likely the name would be considered by the Secretary of State to be offensive, or to constitute a criminal offence?   *CA 1985, ss 26(1)(d),(e)*   ☐

7.   Is it possible that the Secretary of State may consider the proposed name to be misleading as regards the nature of activities undertaken and that it is likely to cause harm to the public?   *CA 1985, ss 32-34* **CSH 2.14**   ☐

8.   Has a search of the Trade Marks Index been conducted to ensure there is no risk of a trade mark infringement?   ☐

9.   Are you aware of any organisations or entities trading under a business name which is either the same as or similar to that of the proposed name?   ☐

10.   Have you considered, whilst looking at the register of names, that use of the proposed new name by the company may cause a company with a similar name to initiate an action for passing-off?   **CSH 2.16**   ☐

11.   Upon the selection of an appropriate company name, has the company passed the necessary resolution to change the name?   **Checklist 7.1, 7.5, 7.10**   ☐

12.   Has the resolution passed by the company been filed at Companies House together with a cheque for the appropriate sum?   **Checklist 5.1**   ☐

13.   If the company is subject to the UK Listing Authority Listing Rules, have two copies of the Special Resolution been sent to the UK Listing Authority?   **LR 9.31**   ☐

Following the change of name

14.   Having filed the resolution to change the name at Companies House, have you received a Certificate of Incorporation on Change of Name?   *CA 1985, ss 13, 28(6)*   ☐

15.   If the company is subject to the UK Listing Authority Listing Rules, have the appropriate notifications been made to the Regulatory Information Service and the UK Listing Authority?   **LR 9.40**   ☐

16.   Have the Memorandum and Articles of Association of the Company been amended to reflect the new name?   *CA 1985, s 18*   ☐

17.   Have the following documents been amended to take effect as of the date of the change of name: *CA 1985, ss 349(1)(a)-(d)* **Checklist 3.10 CSH 2.18**   ☐

17.1   business letterheads;   ☐

17.2 all notices and other official publications; ☐

17.3 all bills of exchange, promissory notes, endorsements, cheques and orders for money or goods purporting to be signed by or on behalf of the Company; and ☐

17.4 all bills of parcels, invoices, receipts and letters of credit? ☐

18. Have the following been amended to show the new name: ☐

18.1 company stationery; ☐

18.2 minute books; ☐

18.3 statutory books; ☐

18.4 entries in registers of other companies; ☐

18.5 share certificates; ☐

18.6 loan stock certificates; ☐

18.7 franking; ☐

18.8 logos; ☐

18.9 overseas registrations; ☐

18.10 title deeds; ☐

18.11 pension scheme documentation; ☐

18.12 trade marks/patent registration; ☐

18.13 long-term contracts; ☐

18.14 service agreements; ☐

18.15 contracts of employment; ☐

18.16 invoices/conditions of sale; and ☐

18.17 phone and fax lists/books? ☐

19. Has the new name been displayed outside the company's ☐
     registered office and any other places of business and is the new
     name displayed on any vehicles used for business and any
     packaging of products?

20. If the company has a common seal, has a new seal been adopted ☐
     (not compulsory)?

21. Has the bank and any other business associates such as solicitors, ☐
     auditors, accountants, holders of any 'charge', insurance brokers,
     patent and trade mark agents and the like, been notified of the
     change of name?

22. Has an announcement of the change of name been made to the ☐
     following persons:

     22.1 staff; ☐

     22.2 customers; ☐

     22.3 suppliers; ☐

     22.4 creditors; ☐

     22.5 Data Protection Registry; ☐

     22.6 Office of Fair Trading; ☐

     22.7 telecom provider; ☐

     22.8 trade associations; ☐

     22.9 advertising/publicity agents; and ☐

     22.10 Inspector of Taxes/Customs & Excise? ☐

23. Have any undertakings or assurances, provided in order to change   *CA 1985, s 28(3)* ☐
     the name, been fulfilled? For example, if the word 'holding' is
     included in the company name, has the company fulfilled its
     obligation to acquire the majority of the issued share capital in at
     least one other company within three months of the change of
     name?

Practical Notes

It is impossible to be certain whether the use of a company name will provoke a passing-off action, so companies need to research and take a prudent approach so as not to build up substantial goodwill in a company name only to be forced to change it at a later date. A passing-off action can be expensive to defend.

A change of name takes effect when the Certificate of Incorporation on Change of Name is issued by Companies House.

It takes Companies House 7-10 working days to change the name of a company and costs £10.00, though there is a same-day procedure which costs £80.00 (correct at the time of writing).

APPENDIX A

You will need the approval of the Secretary of State for Trade and Industry before you use any of the following words or expressions (or their plural or possessive forms) in your chosen company name.

(a) Words which imply national or international pre-eminence:

British	Great Britain	National	Wales
England	International	Scotland	Welsh
English	Ireland	Scottish	
European	Irish	United Kingdom	

(b) Words which imply business pre-eminence or representative or authoritative status:

Association	Board	Federation	Institution
Authority	Council	Institute	Society

(c) Words which imply specific objects or functions:

Assurance	Chartered	Holding	Re-assurer
Assurer	Charity	Industrial & provident society	Register
Benevolent	Chemist		Registered
	Chemistry	Insurance	Re-insurance
	Co-operative	Insurer	Re-insurer
	Foundation	Patent	Sheffield
	Friendly society	Patentee	Stock exchange
	Fund	Post office	Trade union
Charter	Group	Reassurance	Trust

APPENDIX B

Words or expressions in the following list need the approval of the Secretary of State. If you want to use any of them in your company name you will need to write first to the relevant body to ask if they have any objection to its use. When you applying for approval to use the name you should advise Companies House that you have written to the relevant body and enclose a copy of the reply received.

Word or Expression	**Relevant Body for companies intending to have registered office in England or Wales**	**Relevant Body for companies intending to have registered office in Scotland**
Apothecary	The Worshipful Society of Apothecaries of London Apothecaries Hall lackfriars Lane London EC4V 6EJ1	The Royal Pharmaceutical Society of Great Britain Law Department Lambeth High St London SE1 7JN

Charity, Charitable	Charity Commission Registration Division Harmsworth House 13-15 Bouverie Street London EC4Y 8DP	*For recognition as a Scottish charity* *Inland Revenue* *FICO (Scotland)* *Trinity Park House* *South Trinity Road* *Edinburgh* *EH5 3SD*
	*or for companies **not** intending to register as a charity* Charity Commission 2nd Floor20 Kings Parade Queens DockLiverpool L3 4DQ	
Contact Lens	The Registrar General Optical Council 41 Harley Street London W1N 2DJ	As for England and Wales
Dental, Dentistry	The Registrar General Dental Council 37 Wimpole Street London W1M 8DQ	As for England and Wales
District Nurse, Health Visitor, Midwife, Midwifery, Nurse, Nursing	The Registrar & Chief Executive United Kingdom Central Council for Nursing, Midwifery and Health Visiting 23 Portland Place London W1N 3AF	As for England and Wales
Health Centre	Office of the Solicitor Department of Health & Social Security 48 Carey Street London WC2A 2LS	As for England and Wales
Health Service	NHS Management Executive Department of Health Wellington House 133-155 Waterloo Road London SE1 8UG	As for England and Wales
Police	Home Office Police Dept Strategy Group Room 510 50 Queen Anne's Gate London SW1H 9AT	The Scottish Ministers Police Division St Andrews House Regent Road Edinburgh EH1 3DG
Polytechnic	Department of Education and Science FHE 1B Sanctuary Buildings Great Smith Street Westminster London SW1P 3BT	As for England and Wales

Pregnancy, Termination, Abortion	Department of Health Area 423 Wellington House 133-135 Waterloo Road London SE1 8UG	As for England and Wales
Royal, Royale, Royalty, King, Queen, Prince, Princess, Windsor, Duke, His/Her Majesty	*(If based in England)* Constitutional Unit Room 1374 Lord Chancellors Department 50 Queen Anne's Gate London SW1H 9AT *(If based in Wales)* The National Assembly for Wales Crown Buildings Cathays Park Cardiff CF10 3NQ	The Scottish Ministers Civil Law and Legal Aid Division Saughton House Broomhouse Drive Edinburgh EH11 3XD
Special School	Department for Education and Employment Schools 2 Branch Sanctuary Buildings Great Smith Street Westminster London SW1P 3BT	As for England and Wales
University	Privy Council Office 68 Whitehall London SW1A 2AT	As for England and Wales

APPENDIX C

Certain words or expressions (listed below) are covered by other legislation and their use in company names might be a criminal offence. If you want to use any of these words or expressions in your company name, then you should contact the relevant regulatory authority or ask us for advice before proceeding. We may seek independent advice from the relevant body.

Word Or Expression	**Relevant Legislation**	**Relevant Body**
Architect	*Section 20, Architects Registration Act 1997*	Architects Registration Board 73 Hallam Street London W1N 6EE
Credit Union	*Credit Union Act 1979*	The Public Records Section Financial Services Authority 25 The North Colonnade Canary Wharf London E14 5HS
Veterinary Surgeon, Veterinary, Vet	*Sections 19, 20, Veterinary Surgeons Act 1966*	The Registrar Royal College of Veterinary Surgeons 62-64 Horseferry Rd London SW1P 2AF
Dentist, Dental Surgeon, Dental Practitioner	*Dental Act 1984*	The Registrar General Dental Council 37 Wimpole Street London W1M 8DQ

Drug, Druggist, Pharmaceutical, Pharmaceutist, Pharmacist, Pharmacy	*Section 78, Medicines Act 1968*	The Director of Legal Services The Royal Pharmaceutical Society of Great Britain 1 Lambeth High Street London SE1 7JN (for Scottish Registered Companies) The Pharmaceutical Society 36 York Place Edinburgh EH13HU
Olympiad, Olympiads, Olympian, Olympians, Olympic, Olympics, *or translation of these*	*Olympic Symbol etc. (Protection) Act 1995* *Also protects Olympic symbols of five interlocking rings and motto 'Citius Altius Fortius'*	British Olympic Association 1 Wandsworth Plain London SW18 1EH
Optician, Ophthalmic Optician, Dispensing Optician, Enrolled Optician, Registered Optician, Optometrist	*Opticians Act 1989*	The Registrar General Optical Council 41 Harley Street London W1N 2DJ
Red Cross, Geneva Cross, Red Crescent, Red Lion and Sun	*Geneva Convention Act 1957*	Seek advice of Companies House
Anzac	*Section 1, Anzac Act 1916*	Seek advice of Companies House
Chiropodist, Dietician, Medical Laboratory, Technician, Occupational Therapist, Orthoptist, Physiotherapist,	*Professions Supplementary to Medicine Act 1960* if preceded by Registered, State or Registered	Mrs Joan Arnott Department of Health HRD HRB Rm 2N35A Quarry House
Radiographer, Remedial Gymnast		Quarry Hill Leeds LS2 7JE
Institute of Laryngology, Institute of Otology, Institute of Urology, Institute of Orthopaedics	*University College London Act 1988*	Seek advice of University College London Gower Street London WC1E 6BT
Patent Office, Patent Agent	*Copyright, Designs and Patents Act 1988*	IPPD (Intellectual Property Policy Directorate) Room 3B38, Concept House The Patent Office Cardiff Road Newport, NP10 8QQ
Building Society	*Building Society Act 1986*	Seek advice of Building Societies Commission Victoria House 30-40 Kingsway London WC2B 6ES

Chamber(s) of Business,
Chamber(s) of Commerce,
Chamber(s) of Commerce and
Industry, Chamber(s) of
Commerce, Training and
Enterprise, Chamber(s) of
Enterprise, Chamber(s) of
Industry, Chamber(s) of
Trade, Chamber(s) of Trade
and Industry, Chamber(s) of
Training, Chamber(s) of
Training and Enterprise
*or the Welsh translations of
these words*

*Company and Business
Names (Chamber of
Commerce etc.) Act 1999*

Guidance is available from
Companies House

Reproduced with the permission of the Controller of Her Majesty's Stationery Office.

2.9   Re-Registration of a Limited Company as Unlimited

The effect of this type of re-registration is to make the members liable for the debts of the company.

This procedure is an endangered species but far from extinct. It seems to go through phases and fashions. It should only be undertaken when there is a high level of certainty as to any liability of the members. The lack of capital restrictions on unlimited companies is the main reason why the members may consent to this type of a re-registration.

Company Secretary's Handbook reference: CSH 2.54

When proposing to re-register a limited company as unlimited, the following points should be considered.

Task:	Reference:	✍
1. Has the Company previously been an unlimited company (as, if not, it is not possible to re-register a second time)?	*CA 1985, s 49(2)*	☐
2. Is it proposed to change the company name as a whole or simply the suffix (e.g. by the omission of 'limited') and, if it is proposed to change the name, have you checked the availability of the proposed name?	*CA 1985, ss 26-28* **Checklist 2.8**	☐
3. Have you prepared a set of Memorandum and Articles of Association and are these appropriate for an unlimited company?	*CA 1985, s 49(5),(6)* **Checklist 2.1** **Checklist 2.3**	☐
4. Does the company have two shareholders?	*CA 1985, s 1(3A)* *CA 1985, s 24*	☐
5. Have you completed a Form 49(8)(a) signed by all the members of the company?	*CA 1985, s 49(8)(a)*	☐
6. Have you passed a special resolution to re-register the company as an unlimited company?	**Checklist 7.1** **Checklist 7.5** **Checklist 7.10** **CSH Precedent H, Appendix 2D**	☐
7. Has a director completed a statutory declaration in Form 49(8)b?	*CA 1985, s 49(8)(b)*	☐
8. Do you have the remittance fee of £20 (correct at the time of publication)?		☐
9. Have you filed the above-mentioned forms, special resolution, and the Memorandum and Articles of Association at Companies House?	*CA 1985, s 49(8)* **Checklist 5.1**	☐
10. Have you received the certificate of incorporation on re-registration which is conclusive proof of the re-registration?	*CA 1985, s 50*	☐
11. Have you completed the parts of Checklist 2.8 headed 'following the name change'?	**Checklist 2.8**	☐

Practical Notes

A company may not re-register in this way if it is an unlimited company by virtue of re-registration under section 44 of the Companies Act 1967 or section 51 of the Companies Act 1985.

The date on the certificate of incorporation on re-registration is the effective date of the change in status.

2.10 Re-registration of an Unlimited Company as a Limited Company

This procedure is extremely rare. It is usually undertaken when there is an old company whose reason for being unlimited has long since gone.

It is the creditors rather than the members that need safeguards in this type of re-registration as the members will cease to be liable. This safeguard is given by *section 77* of the *Insolvency Act 1986*, the effect of which is that those members of the company at the time of its re-registration remain potentially liable in respect of its debts and liabilities contracted prior to the conversion, if winding up commences within three years.

Company Secretary's Handbook reference: CSH 2.53

When proposing to re-register an unlimited company as a limited company, the following checklist should be considered.

	Task:	Reference:	🖎
1.	Has the company always been an unlimited company previously?	*CA 1985, s 51(2)*	☐
2.	Is it proposed to change the whole name of the company rather than the suffix (e.g. by the addition of 'limited') and, if so, have you checked the availability of the proposed name?	**Checklist 2.8**	☐
3.	Have you prepared a set of Memorandum and Articles of Association appropriate for a limited company dealing with, for example, the manner of the limit of the liability of the members?	**Checklist 2.1** **Checklist 2.3**	☐
4.	Has the company passed a special resolution to re-register as a limited company stating whether the company will be limited by shares or guarantee?	*CA 1985, s 51(3)* **Checklist 7.1** **Checklist 7.5** **Checklist 7.10** **CSH Precedent G, Appendix 2D**	☐
5.	Have you completed Form 51?	*CA 1985, s 51(4)*	☐
6.	Do you have the remittance fee of £20 (correct at the time of publication)?		☐
7.	Have you filed all the necessary documents at Companies House?	*CA 1985, s 51(5)* **Checklist 5.1**	☐
8.	Have you received the certificate of incorporation on re-registration which is conclusive proof of the re-registration?	*CA 1985, s 52*	☐
9.	Have you completed the parts of Checklist 2.8 headed 'following the name change'?	**Checklist 2.8**	☐

Practical Notes

It is not possible for a company that is unlimited by virtue of re-registration to re-register as a limited company (CA 1985, s 51(2)).

The date on the certificate of incorporation on re-registration is the effective date of the change in status.

2.11 Re-registration of a Private Limited Company as a Public Limited Company

This is a reasonably common procedure undertaken particularly when a company is growing and may, at some stage, wish to seek a market for its shares. A public company in the perception of the public may still give the impression of size.

It is often easier to purchase a 'ready made' plc and insert this as the new holding company rather than re-register an existing private limited company as a public limited company, and the audit fee alone may make it prohibitive. Professional advice should be taken prior to embarking on a re-registration of this type.

When proposing to re-register a private limited company as a public limited company, the following checklist should be considered.

Task:	Reference:	✍
1. Has the Company previously been an unlimited company (as, if not, it is not possible to re-register a second time)?	*CA 1985, s 49(2)*	☐
1. Does the private limited company satisfy the capital requirements for a public limited company (currently £50,000, a quarter of which is paid up) and if not is it proposing to increase the authorised share capital and allot further shares?	*CA 1985, s 45(2)* **Checklist 8.1** **Checklist 8.11**	☐
2. Has the private limited company been an unlimited company previously?	*CA 1985, s 43(1)*	☐
3. Is it proposed to change the name of the company other than the suffix (e.g. limited to plc) and if it is proposed to change the name, have you checked the availability of the name?	*CA 1985, s 28* **Checklist 2.8**	☐
4. Does the company have at least two members?	*CA 1985, ss 1, 24*	☐
5. Does the company have at least two directors?	*CA 1985, s 282*	☐
6. Does the secretary of the company have the 'requisite knowledge' and experience, and is the secretary a member of one of the following professional bodies:	*CA 1985, s 286*	☐
6.1 the Institute of Chartered Accountants in England and Wales;		☐
6.2 the Institute of Chartered Accountants of Scotland;		☐
6.3 the Chartered Association of Certified Accountants;		☐
6.4 the Institutes of Chartered Accountants in Ireland;		☐
6.5 the Institute of Chartered Secretaries and Administrators;		☐

6.6   the Chartered Institute of Management Accountants; or ☐

6.7   the Chartered Institute of Public Finance and
Accountancy? ☐

Alternatively a person may be appointed who by virtue of them
holding or having held any other position or as a result of their
being a member of any other body appears to the directors to be
capable of discharging the functions of secretary. ☐

7.   Have you prepared a set Memorandum and Articles of
Association that state, for example, that the company is a public
company?

CA 1985, s 43(2)
Checklist 2.1
Checklist 2.3 ☐

8.   Have you completed Form 43(3)?

CA 1985, s 43(3) ☐

9.   Do you have a balance sheet prepared at a date not more than
seven months before the company's application for re-
registration, together with a copy of an unqualified report by the
company's auditors in relation to that balance sheet?

CA 1985, s 43(3)(c) ☐

10.   Do you have a written statement made by the company's
auditors, certifying that the balance sheet referred to at point 9
above confirms that the company's net assets were not less than
the aggregate of its called-up share capital and its undistributed
reserves?

CA 1985, s 43(3)(b) ☐

11.   If shares have been recently allotted for a non cash consideration
do you have a valuation report?

CA 1985, s 44 ☐

12.   Has the company passed an appropriate special resolution to re-
register as a public limited company?

CA1985, s 43(2)
Checklist 7.1
Checklist 7.5
Checklist 7.10
CSH Precedent E,
Appendix 2D ☐

13.   Do you have a statutory declaration on Form 43(3)(e) sworn by a
director or secretary stating that:

CA 1985, s 43(3)(e) ☐

13.1   the special resolution has been passed; ☐

13.2   the statutory conditions for re-registration have been
satisfied in relation to share capital; and ☐

13.3   there has not been any change in the company's financial
position between the balance sheet date and the date of
application that has resulted in the net assets becoming
less than the aggregate of its called-up share capital and
'undistributed reserves'? ☐

14.   Do you have the remittance fee of £20 (correct at the time of
publication)? ☐

15.   Have you filed all the above-mentioned necessary documents at
Companies House?

Checklist 5.1 ☐

16. Have you received the certificate of incorporation on re-registration which is conclusive proof of the re-registration? □

17. Have you completed the parts of checklist 2.8 headed 'following the name change'? **Checklist 2.8** □

Practical Notes

The requirements for audited accounts mean that most companies have a limited time frame each year for re-registration if they do not want to produce two sets of audited accounts. This is one of the reasons shelf public limited companies are sometimes used and the existing private company transferred to the new shelf public limited company.

Companies House will reject an application for re-registration which does not include a full set of Memorandum and Articles of Association as amended.

The date on the certificate of incorporation on re-registration is the effective date of the change in status. A private company that has re-registered as a public limited company may commence business without obtaining a trading certificate (CA 1985, s 117).

Public companies are obliged to file full accounts at Companies House.

2.12 Re-registration of a Public Company as a Private Company

This is a relatively common procedure. The compliance requirements for private companies are lower than for public companies. Private companies may, for instance, be able to take advantage of the elective regime (see Checklist 7.7). When a public company has been acquired by, for example, another company it is often decided to re-register as a private limited company.

Company Secretary's Handbook reference: CSH 2.52

When proposing to re-register a public company as a private company, the following should be considered.

Task:	Reference:	✒
1. Is it proposed to change the name of the company other than the suffix (e.g. plc to limited) and if it is proposed to change the name, have you checked the availability?	*CA 1985, ss 26-28* **Checklist 2.8**	☐
2. Have you prepared a set Memorandum and Articles of Association and do these, for example, state that the company is a public company?	**Checklist 2.1** **Checklist 2.3**	☐
3. Have you completed Form 53?		
4. Has the company passed an appropriate special resolution to amend the Memorandum and re-register as a private limited company?	*CA 1985, s 53(2)* **Checklist 7.1** **Checklist 7.5** **Checklist 7.10** **CSH 2.52, Precedent F, Appendix 2D**	☐
5. Do you have the remittance fee of £20 (correct at the time of writing)?		☐
6. Have you filed all the necessary documents at Companies House including full Memorandum and Articles of Association as amended?	*CA 1985, s 53(1)(b)* **Checklist 5.1**	☐
7. Have you received the certificate of incorporation on re-registration which is conclusive proof of the re-registration?	*CA 1985, s 55*	☐
8. Have you completed the parts of Checklist 2.8 headed 'following the name change'?	**Checklist 2.8**	☐

Practical Notes

Companies House will normally wait 28 days from the receipt of the resolution before processing the change as pursuant to CA 1985, s 54. When the special resolution has been passed an application can be made to court for its cancellation within 28 days by:

- *holders of no less than 5% in nominal value of the company's issued share capital of any class thereof; or*
- *5% of its members if it is not limited by shares; or*
- *not less than 50 of the company's members.*

If an application has been made the company must notify Companies House on Form 54. However, it is far more likely that all the members have agreed to the passing of the special resolution and if this is the case, and it is notified to Companies House when filing the documents in respect of the re-registration, the 28 day period will be waived.

The date on the certificate of incorporation on re-registration is the effective date of the change in status.

2.13   **Restoration**

The ability to restore a company to the register of companies could be a useful tool available to the directors, shareholders and even creditors of the company when a company has been dissolved (*CA 1985, s 652*), (see Checklist 2.7). This is particularly the case where valuable assets of the company have been discovered subsequent to dissolution.

Company Secretary's Handbook reference: CSH 9.29

When proposing to restore a company to the register of companies the following should be considered.

Task:	Reference:	✍
1. Is one of the following persons applying to have the company restored subsequent to being struck off the register under *s 652, CA 1985*:		☐
1.1 member;		☐
1.2 creditor; or		☐
1.3 employee?		☐
2. Where a company is liquidated have either the liquidator or any interested party applied to restore the company ?		☐
3. If the company was dissolved pursuant to *CA 1985, s 652A* are any of the following additional applicants applying to have the company restored:		☐
3.1 managers or trustees of any employee pension fund;		☐
3.2 any directors who have not signed the Form 652a; or		☐
3.3 the Secretary of State, if this is deemed to be in the public interest?		☐
4. Is it less than 20 years since the publication in the London Gazette of the notice to strike the company's name off the register?	*CA 1985, s 653(2)*	☐
5. If the company was dissolved following an application pursuant to *CA 1985, s 652A*, restoration will be ordered if the Court is satisfied that:		☐
5.1 the person was not given a copy of the company's application for dissolution;		☐
5.2 the company's application for dissolution involved a breach of the conditions of the application; or		☐

5.3   there is a justifiable reason.   ☐

6.   Have you applied to the High Court, District Registry, or a   ☐
      County Court that has jurisdiction to wind up the company?

7.   Have you prepared: ☐

      7.1   a claim form (CPR Part 8), together with sufficient   ☐
             copies for all the parties to be served (retaining a copy);

      7.2   a draft Order, (with sufficient copies);   ☐

      7.3   the necessary court fee, and;   ☐

      7.4   an affidavit or witness statement (with sufficient   ☐
             copies) incorporating the following information:

             7.4.1   the date the company was incorporated and   ☐
                      the nature of its objects (a copy of the
                      certificate of incorporation and the
                      Memorandum and Articles of Association
                      should be attached);

             7.4.2   details of its membership and officers;   ☐

             7.4.3   its trading activity and when it stopped   ☐
                      trading;

             7.4.4   an explanation of any failure to deliver   ☐
                      accounts, annual returns or notices to
                      Companies House;

             7.4.5   details of the striking-off/dissolution;   ☐

             7.4.6   comments on the company's solvency; and   ☐

             7.4.7   any other relevant information that explains   ☐
                      the reason for the application?

8.   Have you submitted the requisite documents to the appropriate   ☐
      court?

9.   On receipt of the sealed documents from the court, together   ☐
      with the Notice of Hearing of the Application, have you at least
      10 days before the hearing, served the Notice on:

      9.1   the solicitor dealing with any *bona vacantia* assets   ☐
             (namely the Treasury Solicitor or the solicitor to any
             relevant Duchy); and

      9.2   Companies House?   ☐

10. Has a Certificate of Service been completed and filed at court? ☐

11. Prior to the hearing have you ensured: ☐

   11.1   any statutory documents necessary to bring the   **Checklist 5.1**   ☐
company's public file up to date are delivered to
Companies House;

   11.2   any irregularities in the company's structure are   ☐
corrected; and

   11.3   any penalties for late filing for each set of accounts   *CA 1985, s 242*   ☐
delivered outside the period allowed have been paid;

12. After the order for restoration is made has an office copy of the   **Checklist 5.1**   ☐
order with the court seal been delivered to Companies House?

13. Have you checked that the company name appears on the   ☐
register of companies?

Practical Notes

Costs are incurred by way of court fees, the restoration charge for Companies House (at the time of writing between £250 to £300), the statutory penalties for late filing and legal fees.

Depending on court listings, it can take some time for a hearing date to be obtained.

The court often imposes conditions on the granting of a restoration. The restoration can be restricted simply to allow the company to complete any outstanding matters, thereafter the company will be dissolved again.

In order for the dissolution to be declared void, an application must be made within two years of dissolution. However, if the purpose is to bring proceedings against the company for damages for personal injuries including any sum under s 1(2)(c) of the Law Reform (Miscellaneous Provisions) Act 1934 (funeral expenses) or damages under the Fatal Accidents Act 1976 or the Damages (Scotland) Act 1976, then the application can be made at any time.

Technically, on dissolution, any remaining assets of the company become the property of the Crown (CA 1985, s 654). Therefore, if you do not have an interest in restoring the company, it is possible for you to agree to purchase the assets from the Treasury Solicitor or the solicitor from the relevant Duchy.

2.14 Overseas Companies

There are two competing regimes for the registration of overseas companies in the UK; the place of business regime, and the branch regime. Registration of an overseas company conducting business in the UK is only required if it falls into either of these regimes.

The place of business regime is long established. Whereas the branch regime was introduced pursuant to the *11th Company Law Directive (89/666/EEC)* so that companies could set up branches in each Member State without the need to produce separate branch accounts (*CA 1985, s 699AA*).

In the Final Report of the Company Law Review Steering Group it is recommended that the two regimes should be unified.

Currently the questions to ask to determine the type of registration are as follows.

Task:	Reference:	✍
1. Is there some physical or visible appearance in connection with a particular premises, a degree of permanence or some identification as being a location of the company's business?	**CSH 2.56**	☐
2. Is this a place of business where the company carries out incidental or ancillary functions to the company's business as a whole (e.g. an administrative office or warehouse facilities)?		☐
3. Is this a place of business that is organised in such a way as to enable a person to deal directly with the company here instead of the company in its home state?	*CA 1985, s 690A*	☐

If the answer to questions 1 and 3 are in the affirmative, you are dealing with a branch registration. If answers to questions 1 and 2 are in the affirmative you are dealing with a place of business registration.

Practical Notes

A place of business has been found to be a 'local habitation' of its own such as an office but not carrying on business through an agent nor owning a UK subsidiary company nor the occasional place of business such as a hotel room.

It is far more common for an overseas company to register as a branch rather than as a place of business.

Place of business registration

Having ascertained from the overseas company checklist that you are dealing with place of business registration (the older form of registration), the following checklist should be considered when proposing to register a place of business.

Task:	Reference:	✍
1. Is the company able to register in this regime or is it exempted from registration owing to it falling into the following categories:	*CA 1985, s 690A(1)*	☐
1.1 unlimited companies incorporated outside Great Britain;		☐

1.2   companies incorporated in Northern Ireland or
       Gibraltar; and   ☐

1.3   limited companies incorporated outside the United
       Kingdom, whose operations only fall into the place of
       business regime, and who do not have a branch in
       Northern Ireland?   ☐

2.   Have you checked the name is available for registration?   ***CA 1985, ss 26-28***   ☐
                                                                     Checklist 2.8
                                                                     CSH 2.59

3.   Have you completed Form 691 containing the following   ***CA 1985 , s 691***   ☐
    information:

3.1   a list of the names, residential addresses, dates of birth   ☐
       and business occupations of each director and the
       name and residential address of the secretary;

3.2   a list of the names and addresses of each person   ☐
       resident in the United Kingdom who is authorised to
       accept the service of process and any notice on behalf
       of the company;

3.3   a statutory declaration made by a director or secretary   ☐
       of the company (or representative as described above)
       stating the date on which that place of business was
       established;

3.4   a certified copy of the charter, statute or Memorandum   ☐
       and Articles of Association of the company or such
       other instrument constituting or defining the
       company's constitution? If the instrument is not in
       English a certified translation is required.

4.   Have you prepared a Form 701(a) to notify Companies House of   ***CA 1985, s 701***   ☐
    the preferred accounting reference date of the company   **Checklist 4.1**
    (otherwise it will default to the end of the month of the
    registration)?

5.   If the company is carrying on business in the UK under a   ***CA 1985, s 694***   ☐
    different name than its registered name, have you completed a
    Form 694a?

6.   Have you filed the documents at Companies House together   ***CA1985, s 691(1)***   ☐
    with a cheque in the sum of £20 (correct at the time of writing)?   **Checklist 5.1**

Practical Notes

All companies covered by the place of business regime must comply with certain obligations of the Companies Act 1985 (see CSH 2.60 and 2.61), (Checklist 4.13)

If a company ceases to have a place of business in Great Britain the obligations to deliver documents will only cease with effect from the date that this has been notified to Companies House. The Registrar of Companies does not currently have the power to remove such entities from the register of companies. It is proposed to give the Registrar of Companies similar powers in this context in comparison to those in respect of UK companies pursuant to CA 1985, s 652 as part of the final recommendations of the Company Law Review Steering Group.

Branch Registration

Having ascertained from the overseas companies checklist that you are dealing with a branch registration the following checklist should be considered when proposing to register the branch.

Task:	Reference:	✎

1. Have you checked the name is available for registration?

   Checklist 2.8
   CSH 2.65

   ☐

2. For companies registered in the EC, have you completed Form BR1 containing the prescribed information:

   CA 1985, Sch 21A, para 2
   CSH 2.64

   ☐

   2.1 the company's registered name;

   ☐

   2.2 the name of the branch (if different);

   ☐

   2.3 the address of the branch;

   ☐

   2.4 the date the branch opened;

   ☐

   2.5 the registered number and identity of the register;

   ☐

   2.6 nature of the company or legal form e.g. public or private;

   ☐

   2.7 details of the directors and secretary or the equivalents;

   ☐

   2.8 the nature of the authority of the directors to represent the company and their capacity to bind the company in dealings with third parties together with a statement as to whether this authority may be exercised solely or jointly with other directors;

   ☐

   2.9 the names and addresses of persons in the UK authorised to accept service on behalf of the branch;

   ☐

   2.10 the names and addresses of persons authorised to represent the company and their authority;

   ☐

   2.11 whether the company is subject to any winding up or insolvency proceedings; and

   ☐

   2.12 whether the company is a credit or financial institution under *CA 1985, s 699A?*

   ☐

3. Have you obtained:

   CA 1985, Sch 21A, para 5

   ☐

   3.1 a certified copy of the charter, statute or Memorandum and Articles of Association of the company or such other instrument constituting or defining the company's constitution? If the instrument is not in English a certified translation is required;

   ☐

3.2   a certificate of incorporation or equivalent; □

3.3   an indication of the charges on the company's property in the UK; and □

3.4   a copy of the latest accounts which have been publicly disclosed? □

4.   For companies not registered in Member States in addition to the information in question 2 have you also provided: *CA 1985, Sch 21A, Para 2(2)* □

4.1   the address of the principal place of business, the country of incorporation, the objects of the company and the amount of its issued share capital; and □

4.2   The accounting reference date and time allowed for filing of accounts available for public inspection? □

5.   Have you filed the documents in questions 2, 3 and 4, if appropriate, at Companies House together with a cheque in the sum of £20 (correct at the time of writing)?   **Checklist 5.1** □

Practical Notes

All companies covered by the branch regime must comply with the certain obligation of the Companies Act 1985 (see CSH 2.66-2.67).

If a company has several branches in the UK it only needs to make the one registration (CA 1985, s 690B).

2.15   Single Member Companies

As *section 24* of the *Companies Act 1985* no longer applies to private limited companies, they may only have one member, whereas both a public limited company and an unlimited company are required to have at least two. However, when the number of members becomes only one there are some additional requirements.

Company Secretary's Handbook reference: CSH 3.3

The issues to consider in respect of single member companies are as follows.

Currently the questions to ask to determine the type of registration are as follows.

Task:	**Reference:**	✍
1. Has a statement been entered into the register of members with the name and address of the sole member stating:	*CA 1985, s 352A(1)(i)*	☐
1.1 that the company has only one member; and		☐
1.2 the date on which the company became a company with only one member?		☐
2. When the company enters into a contract with the sole member who is also a director of the company have you ensured that it is either:		☐
2.1 in writing; or		☐
2.2 set out in a memorandum; or		☐
2.3 recorded in the minutes of the first meeting of the directors following the making of the contact; or		☐
2.4 in the normal course of business?		☐
3. When the company ceases to be a single member company have the following been added to the details of the former single member company:	*CA 1985, s 352A(2)*	☐
3.1 a statement that the company has ceased to be a single member; and		☐
3.2 the date on which the company ceased to have only one member?		☐

Practical Notes

Notwithstanding anything in the Articles of Association the quorum for meeting of the members of a single member company is one (CA 1985, s 370a). However, it does not make sense for a single member company to have general meetings in most circumstances so they adopt the elective regime (Checklist 7.7). Similarly they will usually pass resolutions by passing written resolutions (Checklist 7.10).

Contracts between the company and a sole member need not be in writing if they relate to 'current operations concluded under normal conditions' (12th EC Council Directive, Article 5(2)).

3   The Statutory Records

Contents

3.1   Register of Members

The register of members shows who are the owners of the company. It is essential therefore that care is taken to ensure it is accurate and complete.

CA 1985, s 352 requires every company to keep a register of members for a company limited by shares. Pursuant to this section, a private company limited by shares should ensure that the register of members complies with the following checklist.

Task:	Reference:	✑
1. Does the register of members include the current name and address of each member?	*CA 1985, s 352(2)(a)*	☐
2. Does the register of members include the date upon which each person was first registered as a member?	*CA 1985, s 352(2)(b)*	☐
3. Does the register of members include the number of shares held?		☐
4. Does the register of members include the amount paid or agreed to be considered as paid on each share held?	*CA 1985, s 352(3)(a)(ii)* **Checklist 8.3**	☐
5. Does the register include the date upon which an entity ceased to be a member?	*CA 1985, s 352(2)(c)*	☐
6. Does the register include the amount and class of stock held by each member?	*CA 1985, s 352(3)(b)*	☐
7. Does the register include an additional index for companies with more than 50 members?	*CA 1985, s 354* **CSH 3.4**	☐
8. For companies with only one member, does the register include a statement that the company only has one member and the date on which the company became a company having only one member?	*CA 1985, s 352A(1)* **CSH 3.3**	☐
9. Has Companies House been notified of a location at the company's registered office or another place in the country of incorporation?	*CA 1985, s 353* **CSH 3.7** **Checklist 3.11** **Checklist 5.1**	☐
10. Is the register available for inspection?	*CA 1985, s 356(1)* **CSH 3.1**	☐

Practical Notes

Entries in respect of former members of the company may be removed from the register after the expiration of 20 years from the date on which he ceased to be a member.

When a company is entering a transaction probably the first item to be checked in the statutory registers will be the register of members so ensure it is in order and the supporting paperwork is to hand (see Checklist 3.9).

The register of transfers and register of allotments are not required to be kept by a company but are practically useful to ensure that the register of members is in order (see Checklist 8.11 and Checklist 8.13).

The register of members and the index (where required to be kept) must – except when the register is closed – be open for a period of at least two hours a day to the inspection of any member free of charge and to the inspection of any non-member on payment of the prescribed fee (£2.50 an hour at the time of writing).

A board of directors may resolve to close the register for a period not exceeding 30 days in any year by giving notice in a newspaper circulated near where the registered office is situated (CA 1985, s 358).

For further information see CSH 3.2, and Checklists 8.6, 8.7, 8.8, 8.11. 8.14, 8.15.

3.2 Register of Directors and Secretaries

This register contains the names of the directors and secretary who control the company on behalf of the members on a day-to-day basis. Every member is required to keep a register of directors and secretaries and must notify Companies House of any changes (*CA 1985, s 288*).

This checklist needs to be read in conjunction with the checklist relating to the appointment, removal and duties of directors.

When maintaining the register of directors and secretaries the following should be considered.

Task:	Reference:	✍
1. For each director who is an individual does the register contain:	*CA 1985, s 289(1)(a)(i)-(vii)* **CSH 3.15**	☐
1.1 their present forenames name and surname;		☐
1.2 any former name or surname;		☐
1.3 their usual residential address;		☐
1.4 their nationality;		☐
1.5 their business occupation (if any);		☐
1.6 particulars of any other UK directorships held in the past five years; and		☐
1.7 date of birth?		☐
2. If the director or secretary of a company is a corporation, are details of its corporate name and address of its registered office or principal office given?	*CA 1985, s 289(1)(b)* **CSH 3.15(b)**	☐
3. For the secretary who is an individual, are the present forename(s) and surname given together with residential address?	*CA 1985, s 290*	☐
4. Have Companies House been notified of any changes in the directors or secretaries or in any of the information contained in the registers using the prescribed form?	*CA 1985, s 288(2)* **Checklist 1.1** **Checklist 1.2** **Checklist 6.1** **Checklist 6.4** **CSH 3.17**	☐

5. Does the register include the date of appointment and the date of cessation as a director? ☐

6. Is the register kept at the registered office?

    CA 1985, s 288(1)
    Checklist 3.11
    CSH 3.16

    ☐

7. Is the register available for inspection?

    CA 1985, s 288(3)

    ☐

Practical Notes

Forms 288a-c detail what is required to be entered in the register of directors and secretaries.

A company is currently required to maintain details of all the UK companies that the director has been a director of in the last five years. In many cases this is subject to repeated change. Companies House maintains a useful record.

3.3 Register of Directors' Interests

This checklist refers in broad terms to directors' interests, for example, the shares on options a director holds in the company.

Generally a director has a duty to disclose their interests in shares in the company. However under *CA 1985, s 325* the company is obliged to update the register in respect of, for example, grants of options to subscribe by directors (see also Checklist 6.6).

The issues to consider when maintaining the register of directors' interests are as follows:

Task:	Reference:	✍
1. Has the interest been notified within five days of the relevant date which is:	*CA 1985, Sch 13, paras 14-16*	☐
1.1 in the case of existing interests the day following the director's appointment;		☐
1.2 in the case of subsequent interests the day following that on which the event giving rise to the obligation occurred;		☐
1.3 if the director was unaware of the interest or event at the relevant date, five days from which he becomes aware of it; and		☐
1.4 excluding Saturdays, Sundays and bank holidays from your calculation for notification?		☐
2. Is the register kept at the registered office or if kept at the same location as the register of members has this been notified to Companies House?	*CA 1985, Sch 13, paras 25, 27* **Checklist 3.11 CSH 3.20**	☐
3. Does the register contain:	*CA 1985, s 325(2)* **CSH 3.15**	☐
3.1 the name of the director;		☐
3.2 the information given by the director;		☐
3.3 the day the information is entered in the register; and		☐
3.4 the entries shown in chronological order against eachname?		☐
4. Was the entry made within three days from the date from which the interest is received by the company (again excluding Saturday, Sunday and bank holidays)?	*CA 1985, Sch 13, para 22*	☐
5. Have the following been entered in the register without notification:	*CA 1985, s 325(3)*	☐

5.1   the grant to a director of a right to subscribe for shares or
        debentures of the company;   ☐

5.2   the date the right to subscribe for shares or debentures
        was granted;   ☐

5.3   the period which the rights are exercisable;   ☐

5.4   the consideration for the grant (and if none it should state
        there was no consideration);   ☐

5.5   the description and number of shares or debentures in
        respect of the right to subscribe;   ☐

5.6   the price to be paid for the share in respect of the right to
        subscribe; and   ☐

5.7   the exercise of such a right?   ☐

6.   Is there an index with the register unless the register itself forms   *CA 1985, Sch 13, para 28*   ☐
     an index and is this updated within 14 days of the amendment to
     the register itself?

7.   Is the register available for inspection?   *CA 1985, s 326(6)*   ☐
                                                                                CA 1985, Sch 13, para 26

8.   Is the register available at the annual general meeting of the   ☐
     Company for inspection?

Practical Notes

Where listed companies receive a notification of a director's interest, the appropriate investment exchange must be notified of the information.

The penalties for non compliance as set out in CA 1985, Sch 24 are some of the most onerous. Companies are also required to disclose the interests of directors in the directors' report contained within the annual report and accounts (see Checklist 4.4).

3.4 Register of Charges

There is an obligation for all companies to keep a register of all charges registered at Companies House specifically affecting property of the company (*CA 1985, s 407*).

The issues to consider when maintaining the register of charges are as follows.

Task:	Reference:	✎
1. Is the register kept at the registered office?	***CA 1985, s 406(1), 407(1)*** **Checklist 3.11** **CSH 3.24**	☐
2. Does the register contain for each charge affecting the property or undertaking of a company the:	***CA 1985, s 407(2)*** **CSH 3.25**	☐
2.1 short description of the property charged;		☐
2.2 amount of the charge; and		☐
2.3 name(s) of the person(s) entitled to the charge (except in the case of bearer securities)?		☐
3. Is the register available for inspection at the registered office of the company for not less than two hours during normal business hours in each day?	***CA 1985, s 408*** **CSH 3.26**	☐

Practical Notes

CA 1985, s 406 requires companies to keep copies of every instrument creating a charge that require registration with Companies House.

Companies House maintains a register which can be used as a useful checking facility.

3.5   Register of Debenture Holders

There is no obligation for companies to keep a register of all debenture holders.

However, if the company does maintain a register there are obligations in respect of the maintenance of the register.

The majority of debentures appear similar in nature to other charges, however in other cases they can be similar to preference shares.

The issues to consider when maintaining the register of debentures holders are as follows.

Task:	Reference:	✍
1. Is the register kept at the registered office, or alternatively if it is kept at the location where 'the work in making it up is done' has Companies House been notified?	*CA 1985, s 190 (1), (2)* **Checklist 3.11** **CSH 3.37**	☐
2. Does the register include the required information as set out in the instrument creating the debenture?	**CSH 3.36**	☐
3. Is the register open to inspection, subject to such reasonable restrictions as the company in general meeting has imposed, for a minimum of two hours in each business day?	*CA 1985, s 191(1)* **CSH 3.37**	☐

Practical Notes

The Companies Act 1985 deals with debentures and charges separately though in many circumstancesthey are similar in nature.

The Companies Act 1985 requires a company to maintain a register of debentures but give little specificguidance thereafter.

3.6 Minutes of Meetings

Directors have a duty to ensure that a proper record is kept of both general meetings and the directors' meetings pursuant to *CA 1985, s 382(1)*. General meetings would include, for instance, class meetings, extraordinary general meetings and annual general meetings (see Checklists 8.17, 7.2-7.6. Meetings of the directors includes committees of the board of directors (see Checklist 6.3).

The following questions in relation to the minutes should be considered.

Task:	Reference:	✍
1. Are the minutes legible?		☐
2. Do they correctly state the name of the company?		☐
3. Do they state the date and place of the meeting?		☐
4. Do they state the type of meeting, for example, directors or annual general meeting?		☐
5. Do the minutes state the names of those present and in attendance at the meeting?		☐
6. Do the minutes provide an accurate description of the business of the meeting and decision made?		☐
7. If the meeting was a meeting of the members, are the minutes available to the members without charge?	*CA 1985, s 383*	☐
8. Have the minutes been signed by the chairman of the meeting?	*CA 1985, s 382(2)* **CSH 3.51**	☐
9. Are all the minutes being retained permanently?	**Checklist 3.9** **CSH 3.50**	☐

Practical Notes

Minutes may be kept on computer provided they can be reproduced in legible form (CA 1985, s 723), (see CSH 3.51). However they still need to be signed by the Chairman to be treated as evidence of the proceedings. This could be done by electronic signature pursuant to the Electronic Communications Act 2000.

Minutes of meetings are only prima facie evidence and hence may be contradicted by conflicting evidence. The Articles of Association may contain provisions to the effect that they constitute conclusive evidence of the proceedings.

It is usually the company secretary who takes the minutes of the meeting as it is one of his core duties (see Checklist 1.3).

Special rules apply to members' written resolutions (CA 1985, s 382A) and resolutions of the sole member (CA 1985, s 382B), (see Checklist 7.10). Written resolutions of both the members and directors should be kept with the appropriate minutes.

There is no requirement to show all those who attended the meeting but rather that a quorum was present. Best practice is to show, where practical, all who attended. Most companies are required to list the names of the directors present to be included in the minutes of meeting of the directors (CA 1985, Table A, Reg 100).

It is not essential to state the time of the meeting in the minutes.

It is advisable to include the company number in the minutes of meeting as in later periods a company name may have changed.

The chairman may make amendments to the minutes which he should initial at the time of signing. After that the minutes should not be amended.

The record of the meeting should include the text of any resolutions and the result of any vote.

Pursuant to CA 1985, s 383 a company is required to keep the minutes of its general meetings at its registered office and to make them available for inspection by member (see Checklist 3.9). Members have no right to inspect the minutes of meetings of the board of directors.

3.7   Registered Office

The first registered office of a company is the address specified in Form 10 filed to incorporate the company. The registered office is the place for documents to be served on the company and will ideally be the location of the head office of the business.

Company Secretary's Handbook reference: CSH 2.44

The following is a checklist to consider when proposing to change the registered office of a company.

Task:	Reference:	✍
1. Has the board of directors resolved to move the registered office?	**Checklist 6.3**	☐
2. Is the proposed location of the new registered office in the country of incorporation?		☐
3. Does the proposed address to be used for the registered office allow for someone to locate the registered office?		☐
4. Has Form 287 been prepared and filed at Companies House?	*CA 1985, s 287* **Checklist 5.1**	☐
5. Following registration have the following been amended to reflect the change in registered office:	*CA 1985, s 349* **Checklist 3.10**	☐
5.1 all business letterheads which should be taken to include any fax transmission; and		☐
5.2 all notices and other official publications?		☐
6. Is the company name displayed outside the new registered office of the company?	*CA 1985, s 348(1)*	☐
7. Have the statutory registers been moved to the new registered office and have any notifications needed in respect of, for instance, the registers of members as they are been held elsewhere than the registered office?	**Checklist 3.11**	☐
8. Have you notified the bank, auditors and other interested parties of the change in registered office?		☐

Practical Notes

It is a good idea to plan ahead with a change in registered office. There may, for example, be a lead time to produce new letterheaded documentation (see Checklist 3.10).

The change of registered office takes effect when Form 287 is registered at Companies House. However for a further 14 days a person may validly serve documents on the company at the previous address (CA 1985, s 287(4)).

If, for instance, a court order is served on a company it will be at the registered office. It is very probably the place that junk mail will be received also. It is therefore important to ensure that post received is sorted by a responsible person.

3.8   Execution of Documents

It is important to ensure that a contract has been appropriately executed by a company. This checklist deals with English and Welsh Law only.

A company can only enter into contract by the actions of one or more individuals acting for it. When executing a document it is important to ascertain whether or not it will be executed as a deed, as a deed has to executed in a specific way. In most other instances an authorised signatory may sign a document on behalf of a company.

Company Secretary's Handbook reference: CSH 11.4

If a company is proposing to execute a document the following checklist should be considered.

Task:	Reference:	✎
1. Does the document make it clear that it is intended to be a deed or do the Articles of Association require it to be sealed (e.g. a share certificate)?	**Checklist 2.3**	☐
2. If so is it validly executed as a deed by that person or as the case may be, one or more of those parties:	*CA 1985, s 36A* **Checklist 8.10**	☐
2.1 by applying the company seal;		☐
2.2 by the signature of a director and the secretary of a company or two directors of a company and expressed to be executed by the company; and		☐
2.3 by its agent pursuant to a power of attorney?		☐
3. Has it been delivered to the other parties (there is a presumption that a deed is delivered when it is executed)?	*CA 1985, s 36A(5), (6)*	☐
4. If the document is not a deed and does not need to be sealed pursuant to the articles of association is the person signing the contract a properly appointed agent of the company?	*Law of Property Act 1925, s 74(2)* **Checklist 2.3**	☐
5. Has the person signing the document the necessary:	**Checklist 6.3**	☐
5.1 express authority such as a resolution of the board; and		☐
5.2 implied authority or usual authority?		☐
6. Has the person actually signed the document?		☐

Practical Notes

This note does not cover companies in receivership or liquidation.

A contract or deed which purports to be executed by a company before it has been formed will, unless otherwise agreed, take effect as an instrument binding on the agent or person who purports to act for the company (CA 1985, s 36C) (see Checklist 2.4).

For overseas countries in order for a document to be validly executed the signatory must act in accordance with the laws of the territory in which the company is incorporated. It is therefore often necessary to obtain the advice of local lawyers to ascertain whether the form of execution meets local legal requirements (The Foreign Companies (Execution of Documents) Regulations 1994 (SI 1994/950)).

Third parties can rely on the ability of the directors to bind the company pursuant to CA 1985, s 35A(1) (CSH 11.5).

3.9   Retention of Documents

It is essential to formulate a simple, written policy in relation to the retention of documents to ensure that the appropriate documents are retained. Failure to do so will result in inefficiency both in terms of effective time management and use of storage facilities. The retention of documents may be prescribed by law either specifically or by reference to the period within which the documents may be used as evidence in any legal proceedings or based on good commercial practice. Any policy should provide for regular review of the documents retained and should be capable of being flexible in specific circumstances.

Our intention is to highlight the salient issues for the company secretary in formulating a policy for the retention of documents as well as providing some guidance on retention requirements of those documents which he or she is likely to encounter on a more regular basis.

When formulating a policy for the retention of documents the following checklist should be considered.

Task:	Reference:	✎
1. To avoid duplication, the documents should be retained in a central registry or depository. Have you addressed whether:		☐
1.1 the newer, more frequently used documents should be identified, as these might be better placed in a central registry;		☐
1.2 the older documents which are not required on a regular basis should be identified as these might be better placed in a central depository; and		☐
1.3 the central depository could be more advantageously located off-site with professional providers of storage facilities?		☐
2. Has consideration been given to security arrangements e.g. are paper documents retained in fire resistant safes and cabinets?		☐
3. Has consideration been given to the possibility of maintaining records electronically or on microfiche and:	*CA 1985, ss 722(1), (2), 723(2)*	☐
3.1 are any registers, minute books and accounting records being maintained electronically or on microfiche capable of being produced in a legible format;		☐
3.2 are adequate precautions in place to safeguard against falsification;		☐
3.3 has consideration been given to the rules of evidence noting that in civil proceedings the courts will generally apply the best evidence rule requiring an original document to be produced, (except where an original document has been destroyed in accordance with an established document retention policy), then microfilm of a true copy of the original will generally be acceptable and:		
3.3.1 have the documents been appropriately validated and certified; and		☐

> 3.3.2   has The British Standards Institute Code of Practice for Legal Admissibility of Information Stored on Electronic Document Management Systems been consulted? □

4.   Is there an appropriate and user-friendly indexing facility in place? □

5.   Are there procedures in place for retrieval? □

6.   Are there procedures for disposal such as shredding or recycling by specialised firms (security needs to be fully investigated here) or, in the case of computer records, overwriting of data or making data illegible? □

7.   In the case of accounting records have the auditors been consulted on the storage method? □

8.   Has consideration been given to amending the Articles of Association to include a regulation authorising the destruction of certain categories of documents particularly those relating to the register of members, register of transfers and dividends?   **Checklist 2.3**   □

9.   Has the company complied with the requirements of the *Data Protection Act 1998*? □

When judging retention periods and which documents to retain the following checklist should be considered.

Note that references to retention periods here may be by reference to the *Companies Act 1985*, based upon principals of good or established practice, or practical suggestions based on periods within which documents may be used as evidence in any legal proceedings.

Task:		Reference:	✍
1.	Are the following documents relating to the statutory registers being retained permanently:	*CA 1985, ss 19, 20, 380(1)*	□
	1.1 certificate of incorporation;		□
	1.2 certificate of incorporation on change of name;		□
	1.3 for public companies, certificate to commence business;		□
	1.4 original Memorandum and Articles of Association;		□
	1.5 current Memorandum and Articles of Association;		□
	1.6 printed copy of the resolutions filed at Companies House; and		□
	1.7 signed copy of notices of general and class meetings?		□

1.7 signed copy of notices of general and class meetings? ☐

2. Are the following documents relating to the shareholders and their holdings being retained: *CA 1985, Table A, Reg 28* ☐

2.1 permanently: ☐

    2.1.1 master copy of circulars to shareholders; ☐

    2.1.2 trust deed securing issue of debentures or loan stock; and ☐

    2.1.3 letters of indemnity; ☐

2.2 for the last 12 years together with permanent microfilmed record of: ☐

    2.2.1 share/debenture applications; ☐

    2.2.2 forms of acceptance; ☐

    2.2.3 renounced letters of acceptance and allotment; ☐

    2.2.4 renounced share certificates; ☐

    2.2.5 share and stock transfer forms; ☐

    2.2.6 requests for designating or redesignatingaccounts; ☐

    2.2.7 letters of request; ☐

    2.2.8 redemption discharge forms or endorsedcertificates; ☐

    2.2.9 signed forms of nomination; ☐

    2.2.10 stop notices and other court orders; and ☐

    2.2.11 powers of attorney; ☐

2.3 copy forms of conversion for the last 6 years together with permanent microfilmed record. ☐

2.4 the last 6 years of paid dividend and interest warrants. ☐

2.5 the last 3 years of: ☐

    2.5.1 shareholders notifications relating to dividend mandates, change of address or change of name; and ☐

    2.5.2 dividend and interest mandates; ☐

2.6 cancelled share/stock certificates for one year; and ☐

2.7 dividend and interest payment lists until after the next audit? ☐

3. Are the following documents relating to meetings being retained permanently: *CA 1985, ss 382-382B* ☐
    Checklist 3.6

3.1 board minutes; ☐

3.2 board committee minutes; ☐

3.3 resolutions in writing of the board; ☐

3.4 minutes of general and class meetings; ☐

3.5 written resolutions of the shareholders; and ☐

3.6 written record of decisions of a sole shareholder? ☐

4. Are proxy forms and polling cards being retained for one month if no poll is demanded and one year if a poll is demanded?   **Checklist 7.8** ☐

5. Are the following registers being retained permanently either in bound books or by records maintained in any other manner including non-legible formats which are capable of being reproduced in legible format: *CA 1985, ss 190, 211, 288(1), 325, 352, 411, 722, 723*

5.1 register of directors & secretaries; ☐

5.2 register of directors' interests; ☐

5.3 register of interests in voting shares; ☐

5.4 register of charges; ☐

5.5 register of members (though entries relating to a former member may be removed 20 years after their membership has ceased); ☐

5.6   register of seals; and   ☐

5.7   register of debentures?   ☐

6.   Is the company maintaining accounting records sufficient to show   ***CA 1985, ss 221, 222(5)***   ☐
        and explain a company's transactions such that they can, with
        reasonable accuracy, show at any given time the financial position
        of the company and such that they can enable the directors to
        prepare accounts, and:

        6.1   are accounting records being retained for 6 years for a plc   ☐
                and 3 years for a limited company from the date they
                were made;

        6.2   are the accounting records likely to be required for other   ☐
                commercial purposes e.g. tax and VAT, and if so has
                consideration been given to a longer retention period; and

        6.3   is a signed copy of the annual report and accounts and   ☐
                interim report and accounts being retained on a
                permanent basis?

7.   Are the following other documents being retained: ***Taxes Management Act***   ☐
                                                                                  1970

        7.1   directors' service contracts for a period of 6 years;   ☐

        7.2   powers of attorney permanently;   ☐

        7.3   trust deed securing issue of debentures or loan stock   ☐
                permanently; and

        7.4   trust deeds permanently?   ☐

Practical Notes

Given the current efficiency with which documents may be electronically retrieved from Companies House some may consider it not good practice to retain copies of some statutory returns.

Documents relating to the issue of shares should be retained for 12 years rather than the prescribed period under statute in case of a dispute arising over any such issue (see Checklist 8.11).

3.10   Letterhead Paper

Letterheaded paper means the primary paper used for letters of the companies. Similar obligations apply to order forms of the company. Many companies now carry similar information on both faxes and e-mails and it is best practice to do so.

Company Secretary's Handbook reference: CSH 2.18

When preparing the letterhead paper on behalf of a company the following questions should be considered.

Task:	Reference:	✍
1. Does it include the name of the company including the appropriate suffix (e.g 'Limited')?	*CA 1985, s 349(1)(a)*	☐
2. Does it include the registered office address of the company?	*CA 1985, s 351(1)(b)*	☐
3. Is the registered number of the company given?	*CA 1985, s 351(1)(a)*	☐
4. Is the Country of registration given?	*CA 1985, s 351(1)(a)*	☐
5. If the name of one director is listed are all the directors' names given (other than the person signing the letter or if the name is contained in the text of the letter)?	*CA 1985, s 305(1)*	☐
6. If there is a reference to the amount of share capital, is the reference to paid up share capital?	*CA 1985, s 351(2)*	☐
7. If it is likely to be used for invoicing where VAT will be charged, is the VAT number included?		☐
8. If the company is a charity does it either state this in the name or elsewhere in the letterhead?	*Charities Act 1993, s 68*	☐
9. If the company is an 'Investment Company' (within the meaning of *CA 1985, s 266*) is there a statement that it is such a company?	*CA 1985, s 351(c)*	☐
10. If the company is a company that is exempt from the use of limited in its name, is this stated on the letterhead?	*CA 1985, s 30*	☐

Practical Notes

Best practice is that even if the registered office is the only address shown on letterhead the fact it is the registered office should be stated.

If 'Limited' or 'plc' is omitted from the name on the letterhead (and the company has not gained exemption under CA 1985, s 30) then this could mean that the person signing the letter is personally liable for the contents (CA 1985, s 349(4)).

The above checklist also applies to order forms of the company. An order form might be, for example, a brochure or advertisement that contains a form that customers can use to purchase items from the company.

3.11   Location of Statutory Registers

The statutory registers are the core documents for a company, showing – for example – who owns the company.

The following issues should be addressed in relation to the location of the statutory registers.

Task:	Reference:	✍
1. Is the register of members located at the registered office or such other place in the country of incorporation as has been notified to Companies House?	*CA 1985, s 353(1)* **Checklist 5.1** **Checklist 3.1** **CSH 3.6**	☐
2. Is the register of debentures located at the registered office or such other place in the country of incorporation as has been notified to Companies House?	*CA 1985, s 190(3)* **Checklist 5.1** **Checklist 3.5**	☐
3. Is the register of directors interests located at the registered office or with the register of members?	*CA 1985, s 325(5)* *CA 1985, Sch 13 Part IV* *para 25(a)* **Checklist 3.3**	☐
4. Are the registers of directors and secretaries located at the registered office of the company?	*CA 1985, s 288(1)* **Checklist 3.2** **CSH 3.16**	☐
5. Is the register of charges located at the registered office?	*CA 1985, s 407(1)* **Checklist 3.4**	☐

Practical Notes

Many companies now have computer-based records which may be available over the Internet and so for many companies the location issue is of less relevance (CA 1985, s 723).

Public companies will maintain a register of company investigations pursuant to CA 1985, s 213 together with a register of interests in shares pursuant to CA 1985, s 211.

The above-mentioned registers must be available for inspection for two hours in each working day between 9.00am to 5.00pm (Companies Act 1985 (Disclosure of Remuneration for Non-Audit Work) Regulations 1991 (SI 1991/2128)). The same statutory instrument sets out the fees that nay be charged for copying such registers and index of registers.

In addition members have a right to access the directors service contracts and the minutes of the meetings of the members.

The register of members may be closed for thirty days in any calendar year (CSH 3.7), (see Checklist 3.1).

4   Accounts and Auditors

Contents

4.1   Accounting Reference Date

The directors of every company are required to prepare accounts (*CA 1985, s226*). The accounting reference date is the date in each successive year an accounting period ends. If a company does not change its first accounting reference date it defaults to the last day of the month which falls on the anniversary of the month of incorporation of the company (*CA 1985, s 224(3)(b)*). The accounting reference date also determines when accounts are due for delivery to Companies House.

Should a company decide to change its accounting reference date it should consider the following checklist.

Task:	Reference:	✍
1. Are the accounts overdue for filing at Companies House (as you cannot change such an accounting period)?	*CA 1985, s 225(5)* **CSH 4.5**	☐
2. Will the proposed change in accounting reference date create a period between the start of the accounting reference period and the proposed accounting reference period in excess of 18 months (as such a proposed change is not possible unless an administration order is in force?	*CA 1985, s 225(6)* **CSH 4.2**	☐
3. If you are extending the accounting period for a second time within five years, can you justify the extension by reference to bringing the company into line with other companies in the group or because of an administration order that is in force?	*CA 1985, s 225(4)* **CSH 4.3**	☐
4. Is it going to be practically possible to have an appropriate valuation of items in the balance sheet including stock at the new proposed financial year end of the company (consult the auditors if you are in doubt)?		☐
5. Has the board approved the change in accounting reference date?	**Checklist 6.3**	☐
6. Has an appropriate Form 225 been prepared for filing at Companies House?	*CA 1985, s 225(1)* **Checklist 5.1** **CSH 4.4**	☐

Practical Notes

Private companies normally have 10 months from the end of a particular accounting reference period to send their accounts to Companies House, whereas public companies normally have 7 months to file their accounts at Companies House (CA 1985, s 244(1)).

New private limited companies are allowed 22 months from incorporation to prepare and file their accounts at Companies House (CA 1985, s 244(2)). New public companies are allowed 19 months from incorporation to file their accounts at Companies House. Even if the accounting period is extended in this initial phase the period for filing the accounts will not change. If a private limited company, for instance, extended the accounting period so that accounts were being prepared for the first eighteen months then they would only have four months after the end of this period to prepare and file accounts at Companies House.

It is not possible to change the accounting reference date of an accounting period which has not yet begun though it is possible to change the immediately preceding accounting reference period.

Companies House is unforgiving about the late filing of accounts. One of the most common reason accounts are filed late is because companies do not take into account that the first accounting period starts on the date of incorporation. As mentioned earlier a newly incorporated private limited company has 22 months from incorporation to prepare and file accounts not 10 months from the end of the accounting period.

A company may make up its accounts to a date up to seven days before or after the accounting reference date without altering the accounting reference date (CA 1985, s 223). The period covered by the accounts is a financial year whether it is a year or not.

If a company carries on business or has interests overseas it can apply for a three month extension for the filing of accounts at Companies House (CA 1985, s 244(5)). The application needs to be made before the normal period for filing the accounts at Companies House has expired.

Listed Companies subject to the UK Listing Authority Listing Rules must notify the UK Listing Authority of any changes in their accounting reference date and if extending the period may need to prepare additional sets of interim accounts(LR 12.60).

The Final Report of the Company Law Review Steering Group issued by the Department of Trade and Industry included a proposal that private companies prepare and file accounts within seven months of the financial year end.

4.2   Approval of Accounts

The annual report and accounts of the company are the main source of information for its shareholders. The directors are responsible for preparing the accounts (*CA 1985, s226(1)*). In preparing the accounts it is important to ensure that they are properly adopted by the company.

Reference should be made to the following checklist when seeking approval of accounts.

Task:		Reference:	✍
1.	Has the board of directors approved the directors' report and annual accounts and has this been properly minuted?	*CA 1985, s 233(1)* **Checklist 6.3** **CSH 4.31**	☐
2.	Is the directors' report signed by an officer for and on behalf of the directors?	*CA 1985, s 234A(1)* **CSH 4.32**	☐
3.	Is the balance sheet signed by at least one director and does that director's name appear on every official copy of the balance sheet?	*CA 1985, s 233(2), (3)* **CSH 4.31**	☐
4.	Have the accounts been laid before the company in general meeting (unless it has adopted the elective regime)?	*CA 1985, s 241* **Checklists 7.5-7.7** **CSH 4.31**	☐
5.	Has the auditor's report been signed on behalf of the auditors (if the company is required to have auditors)?	*CA 1985, ss 235, 236; 384* **Checklists 4.8, 4.10** **CSH 4.33**	☐
6.	Has the directors' report and annual accounts (or if appropriate modified or abbreviated accounts) been filed at Companies House within the specified time limits which are (if the period has not been shortened):	*CA 1985, s 244* **Checklists 4.1, 4.11, 4.12** **CSH 4.36 and 4.37**	
	6.1 22 months from the date of incorporation for a new private limited company or 19 months for a new public limited company; or		☐
	6.2 10 months from the end of the previous accounting period for a private company or 7 months for a public limited company?		☐

Practical Notes

The copy of the company's balance sheet which is delivered to Companies House must be signed on behalf of the board of directors of the company (CA 1985, s 234A(3)). Companies House prefers to receive accounts on matt paper without pictures.

The UK Listing Authority in practice imposes shorter time limits on companies subject to the Listing Rules for the completion of accounts. They currently require that the annual report and accounts is published within six months of the end of the financial period (LR 12.42(e)) and that the preliminary announcement is made within 120 days of the end of the period (LR 12.40).

Although the report and accounts may need to be laid before the company in general meeting and filed at Companies House within similar time limits, the two are not linked. If it is impossible to hold the general meeting within the time limit to lay the accounts, they should – following approval by the directors – nevertheless be filed at Companies House so that no penalty is incurred.

4.3   Annual Report and Accounts – the Basic Contents

It is the duty of the directors of every company to prepare a profit and loss account and balance sheet (*CA 1985, s 226(1)*).

The report and accounts of the company provide an important public relations opportunity for the listed company and therefore the quality of the output needs to reflect this. However, for all companies the audience for the accounts will not just be the shareholders but also employees, other 'stakeholders', potential investors and future business partners.

When preparing the annual report and accounts the company secretary should consider the following checklist.

Task:	Reference:	✎
1. Is the company name correctly stated in accordance with the current certificate of incorporation (or certificate of incorporation on change of name)?		☐
2. Are the accounts made up to the correct date?	*CA 1985, s 223* **Checklist 4.1**	☐
3. Have the accounts been approved by the board?	*CA 1985, s 233(1)* **Checklist 4.2**	☐
4. Does the balance sheet state the name(s) of the director(s) who signed it?	*CA 1985, s 233(1)–(3)*	☐
5. Is the balance sheet dated the same date as the board approved the financial statements?		☐
6. Are copies of each of the accounts, directors' report and auditors' report being sent to every member, every debenture holder, and every person entitled to receive notice of general meetings, including the auditors and directors?	*CA 1985, ss 238(1), 390(1)*	☐
7. Has a copy of the accounts (on plain white matt paper, without pictures or shading), with a balance sheet signed by a director, been filed with Companies House, together with a signed copy of the directors' report and the auditors' report, within seven months of the financial year end for public companies and within ten months of the financial year end for private limited companies?	*CA 1985, ss 233(4), 234A(3), 236(3), 242(1), 244(1)* **Checklist 5.1**	☐

For companies subject to the UK Listing Authority's (UKLA) Listing Rules

8. Has the preliminary announcement of annual reports been published within 120 days of the financial year end and is it consistent with the accounts?	**LR 12.40**	☐
9. Are the accounts being published within six months of the financial year end?	**LR 12.42(e)**	☐
10. Have two copies of the accounts and notice of annual general meeting been forwarded to the UKLA at the time of issue?	**LR 9.31(a) and LR 14.4**	☐

Practical Notes

For companies subject to the UK Listing Authority's Listing Rules it is best practice to publish the preliminary announcement within 60 days of the year end.

For companies listed on the Alternative Investment Market (AIM) the name and address of both the nominated adviser and nominated broker should normally be included as the nominated adviser needs to sign off the accounts. In addition, three copies of the accounts will need to be sent to the London Stock Exchange.

See also *all the Checklists on annual reports and accounts (Checklists 4.3–4.5).*
See also *Checklists 4.10–4.12 and Checklist 4.16.*

4.4   Annual Report and Accounts – Directors' Report

All companies must prepare a directors' report in respect of each financial year. *Schedule 7* of the *Companies Act 1985* sets out the matters to be dealt with in the directors' report. There are additional requirements in the main body of the *Companies Act 1985*.

The questions that follow are those which the company secretary should be mindful of when checking the directors' report.

Task:		Reference:	✍
1.	Has the directors' report been approved by the board?	*CA 1985, s 234A(1)* **Checklist 6.3**	☐
2.	Does the directors' report:		
	2.1 state the name of the director or secretary who signed it?	*CA 1985, s 234A(1), (2)*	☐
	2.2 incorporate a 'fair review' of the development of the business of the group during the year and its position at the end of it (probably by cross reference to the operational or financial review)?	*CA 1985, s 234(1)(a)*	☐
	2.3 contain a description of the group's principal activities and any significant change in those activities in the year?	*CA 1985, s 234(2)*	☐
	2.4 incorporate details of important group events since the financial year end, likely future developments in the business of the group, the group's research and development activities and the group's overseas branches (probably by cross reference to the operational or financial review)?	*CA 1985, Sch 7, para 6*	☐
	2.5 contain a statement of any significant difference between the market value of any land included in fixed assets of the group and its value shown in the accounts?	*CA 1985, Sch 7, para 1(2)*	☐
	2.6 contain a statement of any recommended dividend (or lack of dividend)?	*CA 1985, s 234(1)(b)*	
	2.7 list the names of all directors who have held office during the financial year?	*CA 1985, s 234(2)*	☐
	2.8 contain a statement of the interests of the company's –directors in shares (including options and long-term incentive plans) or debentures of the company or its subsidiaries as at the end of the year?	*CA 1985, Sch 7, paras 2 2B*	☐
	2.9 contain a statement of the company's political and charitable donations?	*CA 1985, Sch 7, paras 3– 5*	☐
	2.10 disclose all acquisitions by the company of its own shares?	*CA 1985, Sch 7, Part II*	☐

2.11   provide a statement on the policy and practice regarding payment of the company's creditors and is a number of 'creditor days' given?   ***CA 1985, Sch 7, para 12*** ☐

3.   If the average number of employees of the company exceeded 250 in each week during the financial year, is there: ***CA 1985, Sch 7, Part III*** ☐

    3.1   a statement on the company's policy on equal opportunities for disabled employees? ☐

    3.2   a statement on employee involvement?   ***CA 1985, Sch 7, Part V*** ☐

For companies subject to the UK Listing Authority's Listing Rules, does the directors' report:

4.   Provide an explanation of any difference of 10% or more between the results and any previous forecast or estimate published by the company?   **LR 12.43(b)** ☐

5.   Explain any arrangements whereby a shareholder has waived or has agreed to waive dividends for both future dividends or dividends for the period under review?   **LR 12.43(e)** ☐

6.   Contain a statement about changes in directors' interests in shares (including options) and debentures between the end of the year and a date not more than one month prior to the date of the notice of annual general meeting, or an appropriate negative statement?   **LR 12.43(k)** ☐

7.   Contain a statement about other disclosable share interests notified to the company as at a date not more than one month prior to the date of the annual general meeting notice?   **LR 12.43(l)** ☐

8.   Contain particulars of any shareholders' authority existing at the year end for the purchase of the company's own shares?   **LR 12.43(n)** ☐

9.   Contain a statement of the beneficial and non-beneficial interests of the company's directors in shares (including options and long-term incentive plans) or debentures of the company or its subsidiaries as at the end of the year?   **LR 12.43 (k)** ☐

10.   Present a balanced and understandable assessment of the company's position and prospects?   **CC, para D.1** ☐

Practical Notes

It is becoming usual market practice for details of directors' emoluments and corporate governance statements to be kept separate from the directors' report (see Checklists 4.14 and 4.15).

There is no definition given in the Companies Act 1985 of 'principal activities' or 'significant changes' and so no precise rules as to whether something is sufficiently significant so as to require separate disclosure. Activities that constitute 10% of the total turnover or profits are normally separately disclosed.

If the company has a publicly stated environmental or health and safety policy, a report on the issues raised is often set out separately.

The Political Parties, Elections and Referendums Act 2000 inserted new sections into the Companies Act 1985 dealing with political donations. These new sections provide that neither a company nor its subsidiary may make political donations or incur political expenditure totalling more than £5,000 in a 12 month period. Donations in excess of this limit can only be made after an ordinary resolution has been passed in general meeting of the company approving such donations. The definition of political donations and political expenditure has a broad meaning in this context, for example, allowing employees paid leave to attend duties as an elected councillor would be caught. Several large companies have or are in the process of passing resolutions at their annual general meetings to deal with this issue.

Small companies are not required to disclose in the directors' report, for instance, the fair review of the business, the amount paid as a dividend, significant differences in the value of land, post-balance sheet events, future developments or employee involvement (CA 1985, s 246)(see Checklist 4.7).

4.5 Annual Report and Accounts – Notes to the Accounts

The notes to the accounts provide the detailed information on the figures appearing in the profit and loss account and balance sheet with the intention of making the accounts more understandable. *Part III* of *Schedule 4* of the *Companies Act 1985* sets out the form and content of the notes to the accounts.

This is an extensive and detailed section of the annual report and accounts and the following questions are restricted to issues that usually fall within the remit of the company secretary.

Task:	**Reference:**	✍
1. Is there a statement of the accounting policies adopted in determining the amounts to be included in the balance sheet and profit or loss account of the company?	*CA 1985, Sch 4, para 36*	☐
2. Is there a statement that the accounts have been prepared in accordance with applicable accounting standards (or details of any material departures from such standards)?	*CA 1985, Sch 4, para 36A*	☐
3. Has the authorised share capital and the number and aggregate nominal value of each class of shares allotted been correctly stated?	*CA 1985, Sch 4, para 38*	☐
4. Have details of the number and categories of employees, together with associated costs, been included?	*CA 1985, Sch 4, para 56*	☐
5. Has disclosure been made of any significant holding of the parent company in an undertaking which is not a subsidiary undertaking, a joint venture or an associated undertaking?	*CA 1985, Sch 5, para 23*	☐
6. Is there a list of subsidiary undertakings and are details given of the group's shareholdings in its subsidiary undertakings (if any)? Do the details include:	*CA 1985, Sch 5, paras 15-16*	☐
6.1 the name of the undertaking;	*CA 1985, Sch 5, paras, 1, 8, 15, 22, 24, 27*	☐
6.2 the country of incorporation or, if unincorporated, the address of its principal place of business;		☐
6.3 the identity and proportion of the nominal value of each class of shares held;		☐
6.4 the proportion of voting rights of principal subsidiaries whose results or financial position principally affect the figures in the consolidated accounts;		☐
6.5 the nature of the business of each principal subsidiary whose results or financial position principally affect the figures in the consolidated accounts; and		☐
6.6 for each consolidated subsidiary, including information prepared to a different date or accounting period from that of the parent, the name of the subsidiary, the accounting date or period of the subsidiary and the reason for using the different date or period?		☐

7. Has a segmental analysis of trading for companies in the group which carry on substantially different classes of business or supply substantially different geographical markets been given?   *CA 1985, Sch 4, para 55*   ☐

    If segmental information is not given because it is prejudicial to the interests of the company this fact needs to be stated.

8. For shares allotted during the year have details been given of the classes of shares, the number of shares allotted, the aggregate nominal value of shares and the consideration received?   *CA 1985, Sch 4, para 39*   ☐

For Companies subject to the Listing Rules

9. Is there a statement of any interest capitalised, including an indication of the amount and treatment of related tax relief?   **LR 12.43(c)**   ☐

10. Are details given of any arrangement under which a director has waived emoluments or future emoluments from a groupcompany?   **LR 12.43(d)**   ☐

11. For shares allotted for cash during the year to non-shareholders which have not been authorised by the shareholders, have details been given of the names of the allottees (or if more than six in number, a generic description of them), and the market price of the shares?   **LR 12.43(o)**   ☐

12. Are particulars given of the participation of the company's parent undertaking (if any) in any placing of the company's shares?   **LR 12.43(p)**   ☐

13. Are particulars given of any contract of significance subsisting during the period under review: **LR 12.43(q), 12.44**   ☐

    13.1 which any member of the group is a party to and in which a director of the company is or was materially interested; or

    13.2 between any member of the group and a controlling shareholder subsisting during the period under review?   **LR 12.43(r), 12.44**   ☐

14. Are particulars given of any contract for the provision of services to a member of the group by a controlling shareholder?   **LR 12.43(s)**   ☐

15. Are details given of small related party transactions?   **LR 12.43(t)**   ☐

Practical Notes

For companies subject to the Listing Rules, see also CA 1985, Sch 6, Parts II and III for details of the statutory requirements on disclosure of loans, quasi loans and other dealings in favour of directors and officers of the company and other transactions, agreements and arrangements, details of which might not otherwise fall to be disclosed under the Listing Rules.

For AIM companies the identity of related part transactions, value of consideration and other relevant circumstances must be included if a specified percentage ratio exceeds 0.25 percent. Ratios are normally based on assets, profits, consideration to assets and consideration to market capitalisation (see rule 17 and Schedule 3 of the AIM rules for companies as published by the London Stock Exchange).

Small and medium-sized companies are exempt from compliance with many of the above-mentioned regulations (see Checklists 4.6 and 4.7).

4.6   Medium-sized Companies

Special provisions in respect of the preparation of accounts apply to medium-sized companies provided that the company fulfils certain criteria (*CA 1985, s 246A*).

It should be noted that as part of the Department of Trade and Industry review of Company Law, the final recommendations of the Company Law Review Steering Group include the proposed abolition of the 'medium sized' company as a separate category.

For a company to qualify for the exemptions available to a 'medium-sized company' in relation to a particular year, reference should be made to the following checklist.

Task:	Reference:	✍
1. Does the company fulfil two of the following conditions for the year in question:	*CA 1985, s 247(3)* **CSH 4.20**	☐
1.1 the turnover is £11.2m or less;		☐
1.2 the balance sheet total is £5.6m or less; or		☐
1.3 the average number of employees during the relevant period does not exceed 250?		☐
2. Has the company satisfied two of the conditions in 1. above:	*CA 1985, s 247(1), (2)* **CSH 4.20**	☐
2.1 since incorporation; or		☐
2.2 in that year and in the preceding year?		☐
3. The Company is not:	*CA 1985, s 247A(1)* **CSH 4.10**	☐
3.1 a public company; or		☐
3.2 a banking or insurance company.		☐
4. The Company is not a member of an ineligible group which is a group that contains either:	*CA 1985, s 247A(2)* **CSH 4.10**	☐
4.1 a public company; or		☐
4.2 a body corporate that can offer its shares or debentures to the public.		☐

Practical Notes

If you think your company might qualify as a medium-sized company, we recommend you take professional advice before preparing the provisional accounts.

Medium-sized companies may file a modified profit and loss account and abbreviated accounts at Companies House (see Checklists 4.11 and 4.12).

Pursuant to section 248 of the Companies Act 1985, a parent company need not prepare group accounts if the group headed by that company falls into the category of a medium-sized company and is not an 'ineligible group'.

4.7   Small Companies

Special provisions in respect of the preparation of accounts apply to small companies provided that the company fulfils certain criteria (*CA 1985, s 246*).

The intention in respect of this type of company is to relieve the burden of preparing detailed accounts for companies that do not warrant it. The relevant parts of the *Companies Act 1985* are:

- *Schedule 8* – form and content of accounts of small companies;

- *Schedule 8A* – form and content of accounts of small companies delivered to the Registrar of Companies;

- *s 246* – special provisions for small companies.

Set out below is a simplified checklist for the main category of 'small company'.

It should be noted that as part of the Department of Trade and Industry's review of Company Law, the Final Report of the Company Law Review Steering Group includes a proposed redefinition of smaller companies to include larger companies and details of more simplified reports and accounts which such companies have to prepare.

For a company to qualify for the exemptions available to a 'small company' in relation to a particular year, reference should be made to the following checklist.

Task:	Reference:	✍
1. Does the company fulfil two of the following conditions for the year in question:	*CA 1985, s 247(3)* **CSH 4.11**	☐
1.1 the turnover is £2.8m or less;		☐
1.2 the balance sheet total is £1.4m or less; or		☐
1.3 the average number of employees during the relevant period does not exceed 50?		☐
2. Has the company satisfied two of the above conditions in 1. above:	*CA 1985, s 247(3)* **CSH 4.11**	☐
2.1 since incorporation; or		☐
2.2 in that year and in the preceding year?		☐
3. The company is not:	*CA 1985, s 247A(1)* **CSH 4.10**	☐
3.1 a public company; or		☐
3.2 a banking or insurance company.		☐
4. The company is not a member of an ineligible group which is a group that contains either:	*CA 1985, s 247A(2)* **CSH 4.10**	☐

4.1   a public company; or ☐

4.2   a body corporate that can offer its shares or debentures
        to the public. ☐

Practical Notes

A parent company can only qualify as small in relation to the financial year if the group headed by it qualifies as a small group (CA 1985, s 247A(3)).

There are separate limits to determine whether the parent company of a group is exempt from preparing group accounts (CA 1985, s 248A).

Small companies are entitled to prepare and file either abbreviated or modified accounts at Companies House (see Checklists 4.11 and 4.12). However, they are still obliged to prepare accounts for the shareholders.

Many small companies are also exempt from the obligation to produce audited accounts (see Checklist 4.8).

Pursuant to section 248 of the Companies Act 1985, a parent company need not prepare group accounts if the group headed by that company falls into the category of a small company and is not part of an 'ineligible group'.

4.8 Exemption from the Obligation to Produce Audited Accounts

Certain categories of small company are entitled to a total exemption from an audit of their accounts under *section 249A(1)* of the *Companies Act 1985*. The auditing of accounts is a costly process so the exemption from this requirement can be significant for a company.

Company Secretary's Handbook reference: CSH 4.14

For a company to take advantage of a total exemption, it must consider the following conditions.

Task:	Reference:	✍
1. Does the company fulfil the requirements of a small company?	*CA 1985, ss 246, 247; 249A(3)(a)* **Checklist 4.7 CSH 4.15**	☐
2. Does the turnover of the company not exceed £1 million?	*CA 1985, s 249A(3)(b)*	☐
3. Is the balance sheet total for the year less than £1.4 million?	*CA 1985, s 249A(3)(c)*	☐
4. Is the company a charity with gross income of not more than £90,000?	*CA 1985, s 249A(3A)(b)*	☐
5. The company has not at any time within the year been:	*CA 1985, s 249B(1)* **CSH 4.15**	☐
5.1 a public company:		☐
5.2 a banking or insurance company; or		☐
5.3 otherwise subject to a statute-based regulatory regime		☐
6. If the company has been part of a group, that group:	*CA 1985, s 249* **CSH 4.15**	☐
6.1 qualifies as a small group, in relation to that financial year, for the purposes of *section 249* of the *Companies Act 1985* and is not at any time within the year an ineligible group within the meaning of *section 248(2)* of the *Companies Act 1985*; and		☐
6.2 the group's aggregate turnover in that year (calculated in accordance with *section 249* of the *Companies Act 1985*) is not more than £1 million net (or £1.2 million gross); and		☐
6.3 the group's aggregate balance sheet total for that year (calculated in accordance with *section 249* of the *Companies Act 1985*) is not more than £1.4m net (or £1.68 million gross)?		☐

Practical Notes

Any member or members holding 10% of the issued share capital of the company or any class of share may require the company to have an audit by filing a notice at the registered office not later than a month before the end of the financial year (CA 1985, s 249B(2)).

There is a second level of exemption for companies which are charities which meet the 'report conditions' (CA 1985, s 249A). If the charitable company meets the report conditions it may prepare a report of the company's individual accounts for that year in accordance with section 249C of the Companies Act 1985 instead of audited accounts.

The balance sheet of a company claiming exemption from the obligation to produce audited accounts should contain a statement that for the year in question the company was entitled to an audit exemption and that no notice has been deposited by the members in relation to the accounts for that financial year (CSH 4.16) (CA 1985, s 249A).

Dormant companies are not obliged to produce audited accounts (see Checklist 4.10) (CA 1985, s 249AA).

In the accounts of a company claiming exemption from the obligation to produce audited accounts, the directors need to acknowledge, on the balance sheet just above the signature of the director signing the accounts, their responsibilities for ensuring that the company keeps compliant accounting records and for preparing accounts which give a true and fair view of the state of affairs of the company at the end of the year, and of its profit and loss for the financial year (CA 1985, s 249B(4)) (CSH 4.16).

Companies that are exempt from producing audited accounts will usually qualify as a small company (see Checklist 4.7).

4.9   Auditors' Resignation

The auditor of the company is the person or firm charged with ensuring that the accounts produced are prepared in accordance with the *Companies Act 1985* and Accounting Standards. On occasion, an auditor will resign, for example, should a company be taken over by another company it is likely that the acquiring company would prefer to deal with only the one auditor or firm of auditors.

It is preferable and courteous, if possible, to persuade an auditor to resign rather than go through the process of removing them. However, even when an auditor resigns they have significant powers to bring the reasons for their resignation to the attention of the members.

Company Secretary's Handbook reference: CSH 4.48

When dealing with the resignation of auditors the following should be considered.

Task:	Reference:	✍
1. Has the auditor deposited a letter of resignation at the registered office of the company?	**CA 1985, s 392** **CSH 4.48**	☐
2. Does the auditor's resignation letter include a notice of matters that need to be brought to the attention of the members or creditors and, if it does, has this been circulated to all persons entitled to receive a copy of the accounts within 14 days of receipt of the statement?	**CA 1985, s 394(1)**	☐
3. Does the auditor's resignation statement include the requisitioning of a meeting for the purpose of receiving and considering the circumstances connected with the resignation, and:	**CA 1985, s 392A** **Checklist 7.2**	☐
3.1 has this meeting been properly convened allowing the auditor to speak at such meeting;		☐
3.2 have the members entitled to receive notice received a copy of the statement; and		☐
3.3 does the notice convening the meeting state the fact that the statement has been received?		☐
4. Has the letter of resignation of the auditor been filed at Companies House within 14 days of receipt together with the statement setting out the reasons for the resignation (if any)?	**CA 1985, s 392(3)** **Checklist 5.1**	☐
5. Has the board of directors or the company appointed new auditors of the company to fill any casual vacancy?	**CA 1985, s 388(1)** **Checklist 4.17**	☐

Practical Notes

Companies House prefer to receive the auditor's original letter of resignation with a live signature. There is no prescribed form for this notification.

4.10   Dormant Companies

When a company has not traded in a period it is not required to prepare audited accounts. Companies which have traded may be exempt from the obligation to prepare audited accounts (see Checklist 4.8).

Is the company dormant?

To ascertain whether a company qualifies as a dormant company during any period the following should be considered.

Task:	Reference:	✍
1. During the period in question has the company had any 'significant accounting transactions' – being a transaction required to be entered in the company's accounting records but not a transaction involving:	*CA 1985, s 249AA(4)–(7)* **CSH 4.26**	☐
1.1 the payment of a fee to Companies House for:		☐
1.1.1 a change of name;		☐
1.1.2 re-registration of the company; or		☐
1.1.3 registration of the company's annual return; or		☐
1.2 any amount paid for the subscribers' shares issued on incorporation?	**CSH 4.26**	☐
2. Is the company a banking or insurance company?	*CA 1985, s 249AA(3)*	☐

Contents of the accounts of a dormant company

3. Do the accounts include statements above the director's signature on the balance sheet that:	*CA 1985, s 249B(4)*	☐
3.1 the company is entitled to exemption under *section 249AA* of the *Companies Act 1985*;	*CA 1985, s 249AA*	☐
3.2 the directors acknowledge their responsibility for keeping accounting records which comply with *section 221* of the *Companies Act 1985*;	*CA 1985, s 221*	☐
3.3 the accounts give a true and fair view of the state of affairs of the company; and	*CA 1985, s 226*	☐
3.4 on the accounts filed at Companies House that the members have not required the company to obtain an audit?	*CA 1985, s 249B(2)*	☐

Practical Notes

If a company does not qualify as dormant it may well fall within the exemptions for a small company (see Checklist 4.7).

Dormant company accounts still need to include the basic information in the accounts they prepare although exempt from audit (see Checklist 4.3). A directors' report must be provided for the members, though dormant companies are exempt from many of the general requirements in respect of the content of the directors' report (see Checklist 4.4).

A company which has been dormant for a financial year is exempt from the provisions relating to the auditing of accounts in respect of that financial year. Dormant companies must provide any previous year's figures for comparison, even though there are no items of income or expenditure for the current year. In addition they are obliged to disclose, for instance, the authorised capital of the company. Companies House have issued a standard form of accounts for a dormant company which is not a subsidiary company (Form DCA).

Dormant companies acting as an agent for another person must state that they have so acted in the notes to the accounts (CA 1985, Sch 8, para 5(A)).

Dormant companies accounts must be approved and filed at Companies House in the usual way (see Checklist 4.2).

4.11   Modified Accounts

Small companies are permitted to lodge modified accounts at Companies House (see Checklist 4.7). These reduce the amount of information available to the public. The exemptions are not as extensive as those for abbreviated accounts (see Checklist 4.12). The modified accounts combine certain items in the balance sheet. However, accounts that have not been modified are still required for the members.

Company Secretary's Handbook reference: CSH 4.13

When preparing modified accounts the following should be included.

Task:	Reference:	✍
1. Do the modified accounts include an abbreviated balance sheet together with the following notes:	*CA 1985, s 246(2), (3), Schs 4 and 5*	☐
1.1 accounting policies;		☐
1.2 share capital;		☐
1.3 particulars of allotments;		☐
1.4 particulars of debts;		☐
1.5 basis of translation of foreign currency;		☐
1.6 corresponding amounts for previous years; and		☐
1.7 certain fixed assets?		☐
2. Do the modified accounts include a statement in a note to the accounts that advantage has been taken in the preparation of the accounts of special exemptions applicable to small companies enabling a departure from the provisions of *Companies Act 1985, Sch 4* (with particulars of the departure, the reasons for it, and its effect).	*CA 1985, Sch 4, para 15*	☐
3. Do the modified accounts include a directors' report which contains a statement that advantage has been taken in the preparation of the report of special exemptions applicable to small companies.	*CA 1985, s 246(4)*	☐
4. Do the modified accounts include a statement in a prominent position on the balance sheet or in the directors' report to the effect that the accounts have been proposed in accordance with the special provisions relating to small companies?	*CA 1985, s 246(8)*	☐

Practical Notes

Details of directors' and senior employees' emoluments are not required.

4.12　Abbreviated Company Accounts

Both companies classified as small and medium may file abbreviated accounts at Companies House (see Checklists 4.6 and 4.7). Abbreviated accounts are accounts prepared in accordance with *section 242* of the *Companies Act 1985*. Companies that take the opportunity to file abbreviated accounts at Companies House are still obliged to prepare the usual accounts for the members. Therefore, the production of abbreviated accounts are unlikely to result in any saving in audit costs but rather restrict the amount of information in the public domain. Abbreviated accounts contain less information than modified accounts (see Checklist 4.11).

Company Secretary's Handbook reference: CSH 4.12

When preparing abbreviated accounts for a small company have you considered whether they include the following?

Task:	**Reference:**	✍
1.　A balance sheet as set out in *Schedule 8A* to the *Companies Act 1985*, including details of debtors and creditors falling due after more than one year.	*CA 1985, Sch 8A*	☐
2.　Unless the company is exempt from audit, a special auditors report stating that in their opinion:	*CA 1985, s 247B(2)*	☐
2.1　the company is entitled to deliver abbreviated accounts in accordance with the relevant provisions; and		☐
2.2　the abbreviated accounts to be delivered are properly prepared in accordance with the relevant provisions.		☐
3.　On the balance sheet, a statement in a prominent position (above the signature of the director) that the accounts have been prepared in accordance with the special provisions relating to small companies.	*CA 1985, ss 246(8), 246A*	☐

Practical Notes

The Final Report of the Company Law Steering Group indicated that this is an area of the Companies Act 1985 that will be amended.

Currently approximately 40% of companies file abbreviated accounts at Companies House. The accounts need to indicate whether they have been prepared in compliance with applicable accounting standards and particulars or any material departures from them (CA 1985, s 246(2) and s 246A(2)).

Medium-sized companies may prepare abbreviated accounts, however, these are the same as full accounts except that analysis of turnover and derivatives of gross profit or loss may be omitted. As the exemptions for medium-sized companies are not great, and only apply to quite large entities, the utility of these provisions has been rightly questioned.

Neither small nor medium-sized companies are obliged to disclose the remuneration paid to auditors for non-audit work in abbreviated accounts.

Abbreviated accounts are not required to give a true and fair view as they contain less information.

The special auditors' report does not allow for qualification, so if the auditors cannot give the positive statement in question 2, then the company is not entitled to deliver abbreviated accounts.

The notes to the abbreviated accounts do not need to include any information on directors' or employees' emoluments.

For small companies a copy of the profit and loss account and the directors' report is not required for disclosure purposes (CA 1985, ss 246(5), (6)).

4.13 Accounts for Overseas Companies

There are currently two regimes for registering overseas companies in the UK, the place of business and branch registrations (see below). These potentially have separate requirements in respect of the accounts they need to prepare and lodge with Companies House.

Accounts for foreign companies with a place of business registration in Great Britain

Pursuant to *section 700* of the *Companies Act 1985*, for each financial year an overseas company must prepare accounts, together with an auditors' report in accordance with *Schedule 9* of the *Companies Act 1985* (prior to the amendments of the *Companies Act 1989*), and deliver these to Companies House.

Company Secretary's Handbook reference: CSH 4.28

When filing accounts for an overseas company with a place of business registration, the following should be considered.

Task:		Reference:	✍
1.	Has the company prepared appropriate accounts for the size of the company?	**Checklists 4.6 and 4.7**	☐
2.	Are the accounts for the company as a whole, not just the place of business?		☐
3.	If the accounts are in a language other than English, do the final versions include a translation into English annexed to the original language version?	*CA 1985, s 700* *Companies (Forms) Regulations 1985 (SI 1985/854), Reg 6*	☐
4.	Are the accounts to be filed at Companies House within 13 months from the end of the accounting reference period to which the accounts relate or, if they are the first accounts and are for a period of more than 13 months, the period allowed in respect of that first period is 13 months from the anniversary of the company establishing a place of business in Great Britain?	*CA 1985, ss 702(2), (3)* **Checklist 5.1**	☐
5.	Has the Companies House filing fee of £15 been paid?		☐

Accounts for companies with a branch registration

The requirement for these accounts are governed by *Schedule 21D* of the *Companies Act 1985* (*CA 1985, s 690A*).

Company Secretary's Handbook reference: CSH 4.29

When filing accounts for an overseas company with a branch registration the following should be considered.

Task:		Reference:	✍
1.	If disclosure of accounts is required in the country of incorporation, have these also been filed at Companies House within three months of the date they were first disclosed?	*CA 1985, Sch 21D 2(2) & (4)*	☐

2. If the accounts are in a language other than English do final versions include a translation into English annexed to the original language version?   *CA 1985, Sch 21D 2(4)*   ☐

3. If disclosure of accounts is not required the accounts to be filed in the Country of Incorporation then have the requirements under the place of business registration been applied?   *CA 1985, Sch 21D, Part II (8)*   ☐

4. Has the Companies House filing fee of £15 been paid?   **Checklist 5.1**   ☐

Practical Notes

If an overseas company is a credit or financial institution then different rules apply (CA 1985, Sch 21C).

An overseas company which has a branch registration and does not have to publish audited accounts in the country of incorporation, or a company with a place of business registration is subject to the same accounting reference date rules as companies incorporated in Great Britain (see Checklist 4.1) except it may extend its accounting reference period as many times as it likes.

The exemptions available to small and medium-sized companies and dormant companies are not available to overseas companies.

4.14 Director's Remuneration in the Accounts of a Company Subject to the Listing Rules

The *Companies Act 1985, Schedule 6, Part I* sets out the disclosure requirements in respect of the remuneration of directors. Here we look at the additional disclosure requirements for companies subject to the UK Listing Authority Listing Rules.

The *Directors' Remuneration Report Regulations 2002* (*SI 2002/1986*) are now in force and affect quoted companies. The Regulations affect the annual reports for financial years ending on or after 31 December 2002 (see Checklist 4.14A).

For quoted companies with financial year ends prior to 31 December 2002, the following should be considered.

Task:		Reference:	✎
1.	Does the board report on remuneration comply with Schedule B to the Combined Code?	**CC paras B.3.1 to B.3.3**	☐
2.	Are the members of the remuneration committee listed?	**CC paras B.2.2 and B.2.3**	☐
3.	Does the remuneration report set out the company's policy on executive directors' remuneration? Where appropriate, does the remuneration report draw attention to factors specific to the company, for instance, in respect of:	**LR 12.43A(c)(i)** **CC para B.3.2**	☐
	3.1 the total level of remuneration;		☐
	3.2 the main components and the arrangements for determining the remuneration, including the division between basic and performance-related components;		☐
	3.3 the comparator groups of companies considered;		☐
	3.4 the main parameters and rationale for any annual bonus schemes (including caps) and for any share option or other long-term incentive schemes;		☐
	3.5 how performance is measured, how rewards relate to performance, how performance measures relate to longer term company objectives and how the company has performed over time relative to comparator companies;		☐
	3.6 the company's policy on allowing executive directors to accept appointments and retain payments from sources outside the company;		☐
	3.7 the company's policy on contracts of service and early termination; and		☐
	3.8 the pension and retirement benefit schemes for directors, including the type of scheme, the main terms and parameters, what elements of remuneration are		☐

pensionable, how the Inland Revenue pension scheme cap has been accommodated, and whether the scheme is part of, or separate from, the main company scheme?

4. Are details given in tabular form of the amount of each element in the remuneration package for each director and former directors (with explanatory notes), including: **LR 12.43A(c)(ii)** **CC Sch B, para 1** ☐

 4.1 basic salary and fees; ☐

 4.2 estimated money value of benefits in kind; ☐

 4.3 annual bonuses; ☐

 4.4 deferred bonuses; ☐

 4.5 compensation for loss of office and payments for breach of contract or other termination payments; ☐

 4.6 total individual remuneration during the financial year and the previous financial year; and ☐

 4.7 significant payments to former directors during the financial year? ☐

5. Are details given of share options, including SAYE options, for each director by name in tabular form with explanatory notes, together with market price information at the year end and at the date of exercise, for each combination of exercise price and date, covering: **LR 12.43A(c)(iii)** **CC Sch B, para 2** ☐

 5.1 the number of shares under option at the beginning of the year (or date of appointment if later); ☐

 5.2 the number of shares under option at the end of the year; ☐

 5.3 the number of options, granted, exercised and lapsed unexercised during the year; ☐

 5.4 the exercise prices; ☐

 5.5 the dates from which the options may be exercised; ☐

 5.6 the expiry dates; ☐

 5.7 the cost of the option; ☐

 5.8 for any options exercised during the year, the market prices of the shares at the date of exercise; ☐

 5.9 a concise summary of any performance criteria conditional upon which the options are exercisable; and ☐

6. Have details of any single director long-term incentive plans been included? **LR 12.43(u)** ☐

7. Are details given of other long-term incentive schemes (other than share options disclosed under point 6 above), including interests at the start and end of the period under review, awards and entitlements granted during the year; and details of crystallisation, money value, number of shares, cash payments and other benefits? **LR 12.43A(c)(iv) CC Sch B, para 1** ☐

8. Is there a statement of the company's policy on the granting of options or awards under its employee share schemes and other long-term incentive schemes, with details of and justification for departures from, or changes in, the policy from the preceding year? **LR 12.43A (c)(viii) CC Sch B, para 3** ☐

9. Is there an explanation of and justification for pensionable remuneration other than basic salary? **LR 12.43A(c)(v) CC Sch B, para 5** ☐

10. For defined benefit pension schemes, are the following details given: ☐

    10.1 details of the accumulated total amount of the accrued benefit to which each director would be entitled on leaving, or is entitled to having left, and of the increase (excluding inflation) during the period under review; and **LR 12.43A(c)(ix)(a) CC Sch B, para 4** ☐

    10.2 either the transfer value (less directors' contributions) of the relevant increase in accrued benefit as at the end of the period or as much of the specified information as is necessary to assess the transfer value in respect of each director? **LR 12.43A(c)(ix)(b)** ☐

11. For money purchase pension schemes, are details given of the company's contribution or allowance payable or made by the company, for each director during the period under review? **LR 12.43A(c)(x)** ☐

12. Are details of, and reasons given for, directors' service contracts with a notice period of more than one year, or with provisions for compensation on termination in excess of one year's salary and benefits? **LR 12.43A(c)(vi) CC Sch B, para 7** ☐

13. Is there a statement of the unexpired term of the service contract of any director proposed for election or re-election at the forthcoming AGM, or a statement that he or she has no service contract? **LR 12.43A(c)(vii)** ☐

14. Does the auditors' report cover compliance with the specified disclosures on directors' remuneration? **LR 12.43A** ☐

15. Has the board considered whether the company's remuneration report should be put to the AGM? Has this been minuted? **CC para B.3.5** ☐

Practical Notes

Companies subject to the UK Listing Authority Listing Rules are not obliged to comply with the Combined Code but rather disclose when they have not.

See CA 1985, Sch 6, Part I for other statutory requirements which are commonly dealt with in the notes to the accounts.

The membership of the remuneration committee is often given in the biographies of the directors but should still be cross referenced in the report of the remuneration committee.

Details of the directors' interests in shares and options are sometimes now given in the report of the remuneration committee, rather than in the notes to the accounts.

4.14A   Directors' Remuneration in the Annual Report and Accounts of a Company Subject to the Listing Rules – the New Regime

The *Directors' Remuneration Report Regulations 2002* (*SI 2002/1986*) are now in force and effect for companies with financial years ending on or after 31 December 2002. They will require that the directors of a quoted company prepare a Remuneration Report ('Report') which must contain the information set out below in the format required as part of the annual report. For companies with a year end prior to the 31 December 2002 Checklist 4.14 should be considered.

The Listing Rules also require a Report to be part of the annual report (LR 12.43A).

The content of the Report must also comply with the Listing Rules and Schedule B to the Combined Code, or, in the case of the latter, a statement giving details of where it does not and why not (LR 12.43A(c) and CC Sch B).

In respect of the new regime on directors' remuneration the following must be taken into account.

Task:	Reference:	✎
1. Has a report been prepared on behalf of the board?	**CA 1985, s 234B** **LR 12.43A(c)**	☐
2. Has the report been approved by the board and signed by a director or the company secretary and is his/her name stated in the report?	**CA 1985, s 234C**	☐
3. Does the report cover the details of the remuneration of all those who served as a director during the financial year?	**CA 1985, Sch 7(A)**	☐
4. Does the report comply with Schedule B to the Combined Code?	**CC paras B3.1 to B3.3**	☐
5. Has a resolution approving the Report been drafted to be put to the shareholders at the AGM?	**CA 1985, s 241A** **Checklist 7.5**	☐

The Remuneration Committee

Task:	Reference:	✎
1. Has the Board complied with Section A (Remuneration Committees) of the Best Practice Provisions in all respects or does the Report explain any areas of non-compliance?		☐
2. Is there a Remuneration Committee ('Committee') of independent non-executive directors?	**CC B.2.1 and B.2.2**	☐
3. If there is a Report does it:		
3.1 list those who served on the Committee;	**CA 1985, Sch 7A, para 2(1)(a)** **CC paras B2.2 and 2.3**	☐

3.2	name those who advised the Committee, and by whom were they appointed; and	**CC Para 2(1)(b)(c)(ii)** ☐

3.3 give the nature of any other services provided to the company by that person?   **CC Para 2(1)(c)(i)** ☐

Remuneration Policy

'Director' in this section means a person who is serving as a Director at the time the Report is laid before shareholders (*CA 1985, Sch 7A para 3(5)*).

Task:	**Reference:**	🖎
1. Is there a statement in the Report that the Committee has given full consideration to the provisions of the Combined Code in forming its policies?	**CC Best Practice Provisions Introduction**	☐
2. Does the Report provide a statement of the Board's policy on Directors' Remuneration for the current and subsequent financial years?	*CA 1985, Sch 7A, para 3(1)*	☐
3. Does the policy statement give details of any performance conditions which relate to each Directors' share options or awards under long-term incentive plans ('LTIPs')?	*CA 1985, Sch 7A, para 3(2)*	☐
4. Are the following details of any performance conditions given?	*CA 1985, Sch 7A, para 3(2)*	☐
4.1 An explanation of why they were selected;		☐
4.2 A summary of the methods used to assess whether they have been successfully achieved;		☐
4.3 Why those methods were chosen;		☐
4.4 Full details of external factors (i.e. other companies or stock market indices) used for comparison, and		☐
4.5 If no performance condition applies, the reason why not?		☐
5. If granted in a large block, is the policy on the grant of share options or awards under any LTIP explained?	**CC Sch B para 3**	☐
6. Are any changes in policy from the previous year detailed and explained?	*CA 1985, Sch 7A, para 3(2)(e)*	☐
7. Is the policy on allowing executive directors to accept external appointments and retain payments explained?	**LR 12.43A(c)(viii)**	☐
8. Are the policies on duration of contracts, notice periods and payment in the event of early termination explained?	*CA 1985, Sch 7A, para 3(4)*	☐

9. Does the Report detail the pension and retirement benefit schemes for directors, including the type of scheme, the main terms and parameters, what elements of remuneration are pensionable, how the Inland Revenue pension scheme cap has been accommodated, and whether the scheme is part of, or separate from, the main company scheme? **CC Para B.3.2** ☐

10. Does the report explain and justify if pensionable earnings include elements of remuneration other than salary? **LR12.43A(c), (v)** ☐

11. Does the Report draw attention to factors specific to the company in respect of: **CC para B.3.2** ☐

   11.1 the total level of remuneration; ☐

   11.2 an explanation of the policy on the relative levels of fixed and variable (i.e. performance-related) remuneration for each director; and **CA 1985, Sch 7A, para 3(3)** ☐

   11.3 the main parameters for any annual bonus scheme, including whether capped or not? **CC Sch A** ☐

Details of Directors' Individual Remuneration

Task: **Reference:** ✍

1. Have the amounts given in points 2 to 5 below been udited, and does the auditors' report cover compliance with the specified disclosures on directors'remuneration? **CA 1985, s 235(4)** ☐

2. Does the Report: ☐

   2.1 give full details of all of the elements in the remuneration package, including details in tabular form of the amount of each element (with explanatory notes) for each director and former director by name, including: **CA 1985, Sch 7A, Part 3, Para 6** **LR 12.43A(c)(ii)** ☐

      2.1.1 basic salary and fees; ☐

      2.1.2 annual bonuses; ☐

      2.1.3 deferred bonuses; ☐

      2.1.4 expense allowance chargeable to UK tax; ☐

      2.1.5 compensation for loss of office and payments for breach of contract or other termination payments; ☐

2.1.5 compensation for loss of office and payments for breach of contract or other termination payments; ☐

2.1.6 estimated money value of benefits in kind; ☐

2.1.7 total individual remuneration (i.e. the sum of the above) during the financial year and the previous financial year; ☐

2.1.8 details of any element of remuneration which is not in cash; ☐

2.1.9 details of and justification for any significant payments to former directors during the financial year; and ☐

2.1.10 payments made or the monetary value of any non-cash benefit given to any third party in respect of a director's services as a director of the company or any subsidiary? ☐

3. Share Options.   ***CA 1985, Sch 7A Part 3, paras 7 and 8*** ☐

3.1 For each director by name have details of share options, including SAYE options in accordance with the recommendations of the Accounting Standards Board's Urgent Issues Task Force Abstract 10 been given? Details to be provided in tabular form with explanatory notes, together with market price information at the year end and at the date of exercise, for each combination of exercise price and date, covering: **LR 12.43A(c)(iii)** ☐

3.1.1 the number of shares under option at the beginning of the year (or the date of appointment if later); ☐

3.1.2 the number of shares under option at the end of the year (or on cessation of appointment as a director, if earlier); ☐

3.1.3 the number of options granted, exercised and lapsed unexercised; ☐

3.1.4 for each unexercised option:

- the exercise price; ☐

- the date(s) from which the option may be exercised; ☐

- the expiry date; and ☐

- the cost of the option; ☐

3.1.5 the number of options the terms of which have been changed, and the nature of, and explanation for, the change; ☐

3.1.6 for any options exercised during the year, the market prices of the shares at the date of exercise; and ☐

3.1.7 for unexpired options, the market price of the shares at the end of the year together with the range during the year; ☐

Note: Where the information disclosed in respect of unexercised options granted in previous years would result in excessive detail, it is not necessary to differentiate between options having different terms and conditions. These may be aggregated and weighted averages or ranges of dates presented, except where the aggregation includes options underwater at the relevant date, or the terms of which have been varied. *CA 1985, Sch 7A, para 9*

4. LTIPs. *CA 1985, Sch 7A, paras 10 & 11* ☐

4.1 Are the details provided in tabular form for each Director by name of LTIPs (other than share options disclosed above), including interests at the start and end of the period under review (or start or end of employment, as appropriate, if either occurred during the year), awards and entitlements granted during the year, and details of performance conditions and the period over which such conditions have to be met? **LR 12.43A(c)(iv)** ☐

4.2 In respect of awards vesting during the financial year, are details given of any shares, cash or other benefits received, together with details of the dates of awards, money value at the time of the award and vesting, and the market value of any shares received at the dates of award and vesting, and details of performance conditions applying? ☐

4.3 Are details provided of any single director long-term incentive plans? ☐

5. Retirement Benefits. ☐

5.1 Are details provided for each director, of pension entitlements earned during the year, in the case of 'defined benefit' (final salary) schemes, for: *CA 1985, Sch 7A, para 12* **LR 12.43A(c)(ix)** ☐

5.1.1 any change in accrued benefit during the year; ☐

5.1.1 any change in accrued benefit during the year; ☐

5.1.2 the amount of accrued benefit at the end of the year; ☐

5.1.3 the transfer value, calculated consistently with actuaries' professional guidelines relevant to the accrued benefits at the end of the year; ☐

5.1.4 the transfer value contained in the previous year's remuneration report; ☐

5.1.5 the increase in the transfer value over the year less any contributions made by the director; and ☐

5.1.6 a note can be inserted to the effect that the transfer value represents a liability to the company, not a sum paid to the individual. ☐

5.2 For 'money purchase' schemes: ☐

5.2.1 Details of the company's contributions paid or payable in respect of the director during the year. *CA 1985, Sch 7A, para 12(3)* **LR 12.43A(c)(x)** ☐

5.3 In respect of 'excess retirement benefits': *CA 1985, Sch 7A, Para 13* ☐

5.3.1 the total amount of any increase in the pension paid to any director or former director, awarded after the later of the date on which the pension first became payable and 31 March 1997, which is not covered by the scheme's normal contribution recommendations, and would not have been awarded on the same basis to all members of the scheme; and ☐

5.3.2 The nature of any non-cash benefit improved in this way, and the money value of the improvement should also be given. ☐

Service Contracts

Task:	Reference:	✍
1. Are details given for each director of the date of the Service Contract, any unexpired term, and the notice period?	*CA 1985, Sch 7A, para 5* **LR 12.43A(c)(vi)**	☐

2. Are any details of any pre-determined compensation on termination, together with sufficient detail to enable shareholders to estimate any liability in the event of early termination provided?   *CA 1985, Sch 7A, paras 5(1)(b) & (c)* ☐

3. Is an explanation and justification given where any service contracts provide for, or imply, notice periods in excess of one year, and the reasons for the longer notice period given?   **CC Sch B para 7** **LR 12.43A(c)(vi)** ☐

4. Is there a statement of the unexpired term of the service contract of any director proposed for election or re-election at the AGM, or a statement that he has no service contract?   **LR12.43A(c)(vii)** ☐

Performance Graph

Task: **Reference:** ✍

1. Is there a Performance Graph showing the Total Shareholder Return ('TSR') of the company against a suitable TSR index, over a period of the previous five years?   *CA 1985, Sch 7A para 4* ☐

2. Where the results over five years are not available, does the graph cover as much of the five year period as possible? ☐

3. Are the reasons why this particular TSR index was chosen given? ☐

4.15   Corporate Governance for the Accounts of a Company Subject to the Listing Rules

A listed company subject to the Listing Rules of the UK Listing Authority is required to give a narrative statement of how it has applied the principles set out in Section 1 of the Combined Code. There is no prescribed form or content for the statement setting out how the various principles in the Combined Code have been applied. Companies have deliberately been given a free rein to explain their governance policies in light of the principles, including any special circumstances which have led to the adoption of a particular approach. Non-compliance with any of the principles of the Combined Code by such companies must be disclosed.

Company Secretary's Handbook reference: CSH 6.13, Appendix 6E.

When checking the corporate governance statement of a company subject to the UK Listing Authority's Listing Rules, the following should be considered.

Task:		Reference:	✍
1.	Is there a simple statement of compliance with the provisions of Section 1 of the Combined Code?	**LR 12.43A(b)**	☐
2.	Have the auditors reviewed the company's statement of compliance with the Combined Code to the extent required?	**LR 12.43A**	☐
3.	Is there a statement by the directors that the company is a going concern and are any necessary supporting assumptions or qualifications given, and has this statement been reviewed by the auditors?	**LR 12.43(v)** **CC para D.1.3**	☐
4.	Are the chairman, chief executive and senior independent director identified?	**CC para A.2.1**	☐
5.	Is there a clear division of responsibilities between the chairman and chief executive if not, is this 'publicly justified'?	**CC para A.2.1**	☐
6.	Is there a balance of executive and non-executive directors and are independent non-executive directors identified as such?	**CC para A.3.2**	☐
7.	Are the chairman and other members of the nomination committee identified?	**CC para A.5.1**	☐
8.	Are sufficient biographical details given of directors submitted for election or re-election?	**CC para A.6.2**	☐
9.	Is there an explanation of the directors' responsibility for preparing the accounts?	**CC para D.1.1** **Statement of Auditing Standard 600**	☐
10.	Does the statement cover:	**CC para D.1.1** **Statement of Auditing Standard 600**	☐
	10.1 the requirement to prepare financial statements for each financial year which give a true and fair view of the state of affairs of the company (or group);		☐

10.2 the requirement in preparing financial statements to select suitable accounting policies and then apply them on a consistent basis, making judgements and estimates that are prudent and reasonable; ☐

10.3 the requirement in preparing financial statements to state whether applicable accounting standards are followed, subject to any material departures disclosed and explained in the notes to the accounts; and ☐

10.4 the responsibility for keeping proper accounting records, for safeguarding the assets of the company, and for taking reasonable steps for the prevention and detection of fraud and other irregularities? ☐

11. Is there a statement by the auditors about their reporting responsibilities? **CC para D.1.1** ☐

12. Do the directors confirm that they have reviewed the effectiveness of the group's internal control system, including financial, operational and compliance controls and risk management? **CC para D.2.1** **IC para 5** ☐

13. Is there a narrative statement by the directors as to how the board has maintained a sound system of internal control to safeguard shareholders' investment and the company's assets and how this has been applied in reviewing the company's internal control system? **IC para 35** ☐

14. Do all disclosures provide meaningful, high-level information and do any give a misleading impression? **IC para 40** ☐

15. Do the disclosures on internal control cover the following: ☐

15.1 confirmation that the system is and has been an on-going process for identifying, evaluating and managing the significant risks faced by the company, that it has been in place for the year under review and up to the date of approval of the annual report and accounts, that it is regularly reviewed by the board and accords with the Combined Code; **IC para 35** ☐

15.2 an acknowledgement by the directors of their responsibility for the company's system of internal control and for reviewing its effectiveness; **IC para 37** ☐

15.3 a statement that the internal control system is designed to manage rather than eliminate the risk of failure to achieve business objectives, and can only provide reasonable (not absolute) assurance against material misstatement or loss; **IC para 37** ☐

15.4 an explanation of the process of reviewing the system; **IC para 38** ☐

15.5 an explanation of how the directors have dealt with material internal control aspects of any significant problems revealed in the annual report and accounts; **IC para 38** ☐

15.6	where appropriate, an explanation as to why it has not been possible for the board to make one or more of the disclosures listed above; and	**IC para 39**	☐
15.7	details of any material joint ventures and associates which have not been dealt with as a part of the group for the purposes of applying the internal control system?	**IC para 41**	☐
16.	Are the members of the audit committee named, and is it constituted of at least three non-executive directors?	**CC para D.3.1**	☐

Practical Notes

There have now been many suggested definitions of an independent non-executive director. We would recommend that companies look at the recommendation of the Association of British Insurers and National Association of Pension Funds. The statement is currently available at: http://www.napf.co.uk. This is an area which will develop as a result of the current consultation process on non-executive directors chaired by Derek Higgs.

The biographical details of directors are not usually provided in the corporate governance statement but elsewhere in the accounts.

It is advisable that directors avoid expressing any form of opinion on the effectiveness of the control systems of the company.

The statement on risks and internal controls has become one of the more significant parts of the report and accounts so an appropriate emphasis should be given to the drafting.

The 'IC' references above relate to the Internal Control guidance for directors on the Combined Code issued by the Institute of Chartered Accountants in England and Wales.

4.16   Issuing Summary Financial Statements

As an alternative to sending copies of the company's annual accounts, directors' report and auditors' report to all members, a listed company may reduce the amount of paperwork required and instead send a summary financial statement to those persons entitled to receive them. The information contained in the summary financial statement is derived from the annual accounts and the directors' reports.

Summary financial statements have been used by only a relatively small number of companies. Electronic communication is likely to change the practicalities of circulation of large amounts of information.

Here we are looking at how to comply with the regulations to issue summary financial information. Interested parties may view the last report and accounts over the Internet at their convenience.

When considering whether to issue summary financial statements to the members the following should be considered.

Task:		Reference:	✎
1.	Is the company a listed company?	*CA 1985, s 251(1)* **CSH 4.40**	☐
2.	Has the company ascertained that entitled persons do not wish to continue to receive copies of the full accounts?	*CA 1985, s 251(2)* **CSH 4.40**	☐
3.	Has the time limit for filing full accounts expired?	*CA 1985, s 244*	☐
4.	Has the summary financial statement been approved by the board?	*CA 1985, s 233(1)*	☐
5.	Do the summary statements contain prominent statements that:	*CA 1985, ss 251(2), (4)*	☐
5.1	entitled persons have a right to receive a full report and accounts if they so wish and the mechanism for doing so?		☐
5.2	this is only a summary statement of information in the company's annual accounts and directors' report;		☐
5.3	in the auditors' opinion the summary statement is consistent with the full report and accounts and complies with *CA 1985, s 251*; and		☐
5.4	the full accounts were not qualified (pursuant to *CA 1985, s 237(2)-(3)*) or unqualified, and if they were qualified an explanation?		☐
6.	Have full sets of reports and accounts been circulated to those who do not wish to receive only the summary financial statements?	*CA 1985, s 251(2)*	☐

Practical Notes

The Companies (Summary Financial Statement) Regulations 1995 (SI 1995/2092) prescribe the manner in which the wishes of entitled persons can be ascertained so as to establish whether or not they receive summary statements.

CA 1985, s 238(1) sets out that an entitled person is someone who would apart from this section be entitled to receive the report and account of a company (e.g. members, directors, auditors and debenture holders).

4.17   Appointment of Auditors

The auditor of the company is the person or firm charged with reporting on whether the accounts produced are prepared in accordance with the *Companies Act 1985* and Accounting Standards. Some companies do not need to appoint an auditor, for example, dormant companies (see Checklists 4.8 and 4.10).

In relation to the appointment of auditors, the following checklist should be considered.

Task:	Reference:	✎
1. Is this a company that is exempt from the need to appoint auditors?	**CA 1985, s 249A** **Checklists 4.8 and 4.10**	☐
2. Was the first auditor appointed by the board of directors to hold office until the conclusion of the first annual general meeting?	**CA 1985, s 385(3)** **Checklist 6.3** **CSH Precedent B, Appendix 4A**	☐
3. Has the company appointed or re-appointed auditors at each general meeting at which accounts have been laid?	**CA 1985, s 385(2)** **Checklist 7.1** **CSH 4.42 & Precedent C, appendix 4A**	☐
4. Is the person or entity eligible to be an auditor as they are:	**CSH 4.43**	☐
4.1 a member of a recognised supervisory body (that is recognised by the Secretary of State); and	*CA 1989, s 31*	☐
4.2 eligible for the appointment under the rules of that body; and		☐
4.3 not an officer or employee of the company; and	*CA 1989, s 27(1)*	☐
4.4 not a partner or employee of an officer or employee of the company nor a partnership where an officer or employee of the company is a partner; and	**CSH 4.45**	☐
4.5 not connected with the company or an associated undertaking?	*CA 1989, s 27(2)*	☐
5. Has the company dispensed with the obligation to appoint auditors annually?	**CA 1985, s 386** **Checklist 7.7**	☐
6. If the auditor has been appointed to fill a casual vacancy, has either the board, or the members of the company in general meeting, approved the appointment?	**CA 1985, s385(2), s 388** **Checklists 6.3 and 7.4**	☐

Practical Notes

There is no requirement to notify Companies House of the appointment of auditors.

Section 25 of the Companies Act 1989 sets out who should be considered a 'registered auditor'. This gave effect to the Eighth EC Company Law Directive. The bodies of accountants which are designated as recognised supervisory bodies and are suitable to be appointed auditors are broadly the Institutes of Chartered Accountants in England and Wales (ICAEW), the Institute of Chartered Accountants of Scotland (ICAS), the Association of

Chartered Certified Accountants (ACCA), the Institute of Chartered Accountants in Ireland (ICAI) and the Association of Authorised Public Accountants. Registered auditors need to be members of a recognised supervisory body and eligible for appointment under the rules of that body. The recognised supervisory bodies maintain and provide surveillance of these registered auditors. It is no longer sufficient simply to be a member of a recognised supervisory body.

If a casual vacancy of the auditors is filled during the year, special notice is required for the resolution to re-appoint the new auditors at the next annual general meeting of the company (see Checklist 7.11) (CA 1985, s 388(3)(b)). The auditors who resigned during the year also need to be given notice of this resolution (CA 1985, s 388(4)).

4.18   Removal of Auditors

In practice it is rare for a company to remove an auditor. It is more usual and courteous to ask them to resign voluntary (see Checklist 4.9) and then for the directors to resolve to appoint a new firm to fill the vacancy. If the auditors are not willing to resign then it could be left to the next meeting at which accounts are laid before the members, as the auditor will retire at that time anyway (although a large number of companies have adopted the elective regime where automatic retirement does not apply). The same procedure will be used even if a change is made at the general meeting at which the auditors re-appointment would otherwise be proposed.

To remove the auditors of a company from office the following should be considered.

Task:	Reference:	✍
1. Has special notice been given to the company of a proposed resolution to remove the auditor at a general meeting of the company?	*CA 1985, s 391A(1)* **Checklist 7.11** **CSH 4.48; 7.40; Precedent E, Appendix 4A**	☐
2. Has the auditor been notified of the receipt by the company of special notice proposing their removal?	*CA 1985, s 391A(2)*	☐
3. Has the auditor made representations in writing to the company and requested that these be circulated to the members and has this been circulated to the members?	*CA 1985, 391A(4)*	☐
4. If the representations have been received by the company too late for circulation, has the auditor either required that the representations be read out or has provision been made for the auditor to be heard at the meeting to consider their removal?	*CA 1985, s 391A(5)*	☐
5. Has the ordinary resolution to remove the auditors been properly passed?	**Checklist 7.5**	☐
6. Has the auditor being removed been informed of their removal after the passing of the resolution removing them as auditors?		☐
7. Has notification been given to Companies House of the removal of the auditor in the prescribed form within 14 days of the passing of the resolution?	*CA 1985, s 391(2)* **Checklist 5.1**	☐

Practical Notes

The outgoing auditor does have a right of access to the books and accounts of the company and is entitled to require from the offices such information and explanation as it thinks necessary for the performance of its duties (CA 1985, s 389A(1)).

A written resolution may not be used to remove an auditor (CA 1985, s 391).

5   Disclosure and Reporting Requirements

Contents

5.1   Companies House

Companies House is an Executive Agency of the Department of Trade and Industry and provides two services:

- the incorporation, re-registration and striking off of companies and the registration of documents required to be filed by, for instance, the *Companies Act 1985*; and

- the provision of information to the public about registered companies.

When preparing to file documents at Companies House the following checklist should be considered.

Task:	Reference:	✍
1. Has the document been executed appropriately (usually by one or more of the current officers of the company) and countersigned if necessary?		☐
2. Has the document been dated?		☐
3. Is it on A4 paper?		☐
4. Is it on matt paper without any pictures?		☐
5. Do you require confirmation of safe receipt from Companies House?		☐

Practical Notes

The usual way of obtaining a receipt from Companies House confirming they have received documents is to enclose a copy letter, together with a stamped addressed envelope when filing documents, which Companies House will then stamp and return to you.

It may take some time for a document to be processed at Companies House. It takes a day for it to be sorted in the post room and, at times of high volumes, several days for the document to be examined.

You can tell when a document has been received by logging on the Companies House Direct service at www.companieshouse.gov.uk and obtaining a filing history. Documents that are not yet available online are shown in red.

Only current serving officers of the company at the time of completion of the document should sign documents on behalf of the company. The practice of nominee companies of incorporation agents signing their own resignations, for example, is incorrect.

Companies House are helpful and are willing to assist with telephone queries in respect of, for example, the filing of a document. They have specialist sections dealing with capital issues, overseas companies, restorations of companies and charges, amongst others. Their practical advice on the documentation which they would expect to receive can be invaluable. In addition, they provide a number of useful brochures on a variety of topics including limited liability partnerships and overseas companies. Their website at www.companieshouse.gov.uk provides access to these, many statutory forms and basic information on companies registered at Companies House.

CSH Appendix 5D lists all the forms specified for returns to Companies House.

The main address for correspondence with Companies House is:

Crown Way, Cardiff CF14 3UZ.

Companies House also has offices at:

37 Castle Terrace, Edinburgh EH1 2EB
Central Library, Chamberlain Sq Birmingham, B3 3HQ
25 Queen St, Leeds LS1 2TW
75 Mosley St, Manchester M2 3HR

5.2 The Annual Return

Companies House require each registered private limited company to file at least two documents each year; the annual accounts and the annual return. The annual accounts have been dealt with in some detail in other checklists. This checklist will, therefore, concentrate on the annual return.

The annual returns of the company should include the following.

Task:		Reference:	✎
1.	The name of the company and its registered office address (which must be the same as that registered with Companies House).	*CA 1985, s 364(1)(a)*	☐
2.	Details of where the register of members and the register of debentures are held, if this is different than the registered office of the company.	*CA 1985, ss 364(1)(g),(h)*	☐
3.	Information up to a date which corresponds with either the date of incorporation, the anniversary of the last return or such earlier date as the company has adopted.	*CA 1985, s 363(1)*	☐
4.	The company's activity code.	*CA 1985, s 364(1)(6)*	☐
5.	Details of the current directors and secretary.	*CA 1985, ss 364(1)(c), (d)*	☐
6.	Details of the total issued share capital (which must correspond with the total number of shares shown as being in issue in the schedule detailing the shareholders).	*CA 1985, ss 364A(2), (3)*	☐
7.	The names and addresses of shareholders who have transferred shares since the date of the last return, together with details of the number and class(es) of shares transferred.	*CA 1985, s 364A(4)*	☐
8.	A full list of shareholders and their respective addresses, together with details of the number and class(es) of shares held.	*CA 1985, s 364A(4)*	☐
9.	The return needs to be signed and dated by a serving officer of the company.		☐
10.	Following completion the return needs to be filed at Companies House within 28 days of the period end, together with a cheque in the sum of £15.	**Checklist 5.1**	☐

Practical Notes

Companies House issue a shuttle annual return about three weeks before the return is due for filing. However this form needs to be carefully checked especially, for instance, the list of shareholders as there may well have been a share transfer since the date of the last return of which Companies House will be unaware.

Companies House issue a list of activity codes for companies with the shuttle annual return.

If the company has a large number of shareholders (which will usually be the case with listed companies), Companies House will accept a bulk list of members and transfers during the previous year in a microfiche or computerised format.

At the Companies House website (www.companieshouse.gov.uk), you can check the name, number and registered office of a company, together with the annual return date for such company, without having to make any payment.

There is a move towards electronic filing of documents at Companies House and it is possible to file the annual return electronically.

5.3 Companies House Fees

The *Companies Act 1985* grants the Registrar of Companies the power to levy charges in certain circumstances. The fees are specified in Statutory Instruments from time to time and are currently – at the time of writing – as follows:

UK Companies	Charge (£)	Same Day Charge (£)	Relevant Checklists
Formation Fee	20	80	Checklist 2.4
Change of Name	10	80	Checklist 2.8
Annual Return	15	-	Checklist 5.2
Re-registrations	20	80	Checklists 2.9-2.12
Duplicate Certificates	25	60	

Overseas Companies	Charge (£)	Same Day Charge (£)	Relevant Checklists
Registration of either a Branch or a Place of Business	20	80	Checklist 2.14
Registration of accounts	15	-	Checklist 4.13

Limited Liability Partnerships	Charge (£)	Same Day Charge (£)	Relevant Checklists
Registration	95	-	Checklist 2.5
Annual Return	35	-	
Change of Name	20	-	

Practical Notes

The above is only a summary of the current charges in force. The above charges are subject to change so if in doubt contact Companies House. There are additional charges for retrieval of information. Access is allowed at a charge to scanned images of documents they have received and summary information on, for instance, officers appointed and the mortgage register (see Checklist 5.1). Companies House allow access to certain information free of charge.

6   Directors

Contents

6.1   Appointment of a Director

Directors are necessary for the day-to-day running of a company (see Checklist 6.2). The directors are, for example, required to execute the most important documents on behalf of a company (see Checklist 3.8). It is, therefore, essential they are validly appointed.

Form 10, filed by a company on incorporation, provides for the appointment of the first directors of the company. This checklist concentrates on the procedure for further appointments. Such a procedure is defined by a company's Articles of Association. It is important that the Articles of a company are specifically checked especially in relation to age limits for directors or the requirement for a director to hold shares in the company.

The following should be considered when dealing with the appointment of a new director.

Task:	Reference:	✍
1. Is the person an undischarged bankrupt, suffering from a mental disorder, or a disqualified director?		☐
2. Has the appointment been approved in accordance with the Articles of Association (usually by the board of directors)?	**Checklist 2.3**	☐
3. For listed companies which are subject to the UK Listing Authority's Listing Rules, has the appointment been announced without delay?	**LR 16.7**	☐
4. Has the director consented to act as a director, by the director completing and signing Form 288a (which will require details of the director's full name, date of birth, residential address, any former names, UK directorships in the last five years, occupation and nationality)?	*CA 1985, s 289*	☐
5. Has Form 288a been submitted to Companies House?	*CA 1985, s 288(2)* **Checklist 5.1**	☐
6. Has the register of directors been updated to reflect the appointment of a new director?	*CA 1985, s 288(1)* **Checklist 3.2**	☐
7. Have you checked the Articles of Association to see if there is, for instance, a maximum number of directors allowed, or an age limit, or a requirement for directors to own shares in the company and, if so, have these requirements been complied with?	**Checklist 2.3**	☐
8. Are you aware of any interests in shares in the company that the director needs to notify the company of and, if so, has the register of directors' interests been updated and, if a listed company, has this interest been announced in the appropriate manner?	*CA 1985, s 324, Sch 13* **Checklists 3.3, 6.6**	☐
9. Are you are aware of any interests in contracts that the director needs to notify the company and, if so, have you arranged that these are disclosed at the first board meeting at which the director attends?	*CA 1985, s 317*	☐
10. Do you need to alter the company's directors' and officers' liability insurance?		☐

11. Has the Inland Revenue been informed of the appointment of the additional director? ☐

12. Do the directors' names appear on the company letterhead? If so, this will need amending to include the new director. **Checklist 3.10** ☐

13. Is a new director being appointed to replace a former director and, if so, has the resignation/removal of the former director been dealt with appropriately? **Checklist 6.4** ☐

14. Will the new director need a service contract? ☐

15. Have you put in place a procedure to ensure that the director receives notice of future meetings of the board of directors? **Checklist 6.3** ☐

16. Have you informed the bank of the new appointment and, if necessary, changed the company's bank mandate and obtained any specimen signatures required? ☐

Practical Notes

Companies often have a new director's pack consisting of:

- *a letter outlining the duties of directors;*
- *service contract;*
- *Memorandum and Articles of Association;*
- *details of any pension and option schemes; and*
- *Form 288.*

The Companies Act 1985 does not recognise any difference between executive and non-executive directors. They are deemed to rank equally and are thus exposed to similar liabilities.

It is possible an individual may be considered a 'shadow' director even if s/he has not been through the above-mentioned process if s/he is person on whose direction or instruction the directors are accustomed to act. A person is not deemed to be a shadow director however by reason only that the directors act on advice given by him/her in a professional capacity (CA 1985, s 741).

6.2   Directors' Duties

The directors are responsible for managing the company on behalf of the members.

Unfortunately, there is currently no codification of the duties and responsibilities of directors. Such codification has been proposed as part of the Company Law Review currently being undertaken by the Department of Trade and Industry but, in the meantime, the law relating to director's duties is set out in a variety of sources, in particular, the *Companies Act 1985*, the *Insolvency Act 1986* and in an extensive and complex body of case law. Furthermore, a company's Memorandum and Articles of Association will usually include some provisions relating to the powers of a company (and thus of its directors). This makes a comprehensive checklist on this subject difficult.

Notwithstanding the above, directors' duties can, generally speaking, be divided into two categories: duties of honesty and good faith (known as fiduciary duties) and duties of care and skill, and we have separated this checklist into these categories.

Fiduciary Duties

Company Secretary's Handbook reference: CSH 6.24

A director should be asking him/herself the following in respect of fiduciary duties.

Task:	Reference:	✎
1. Are you acting in what you believe to be the best interests of the company (including duties towards employees)?	*CA 1985 ss 309, 719*	☐
2. Are you using your powers for the proper purpose for which they were conferred?		☐
3. Are you acting within the law and the company's powers as conferred on the directors by the Memorandum and Articles of Association?	**Checklists 2.1, 2.3**	☐
4. Do you have a conflict of interest, for example:	*CA 1985, ss 317, 320, 330* **Financial Services and Markets Act 2000 ss 118-131**	☐
4.1 are you taking advantage of your position as a director;		☐
4.2 are you making a personal profit;		☐
4.3 have you informed the other directors of your interests;		☐
4.4 are you engaged in a substantial property transaction;		☐
4.5 is this a loan to a director; or		☐
4.6 is this market abuse?		☐

Duties of Skill and Care

In contrast with the extensive fiduciary duties, which, for the most part impose negative obligations on the directors (i.e. an obligation *not* to do anything which conflicts with the director's duty to the company), there are limited positive obligations and duties imposed on directors (e.g. to require them to actively promote the company). The leading case on the subject of a director's positive obligations (*Re City Equitable Fire Insurance Co Ltd, 1925*), which remains the basis of current law, held that a director has a positive obligation to act with skill and care.

This case established three propositions to be considered in respect of directors.

Task:	Reference:	✍
1. Is the director showing a level of performance of his duties that one might reasonably expect from a person of his knowledge and experience?		☐
2. Has the director attended board meetings (a director is not obliged to attend all meetings but should when he reasonably can)?		☐
3. Has the director properly delegated his authority in accordance with the Articles of Association?		☐

Miscellaneous Statutory Duties

Company Secretary's Handbook reference: CSH 6.26

As well as the general duties of good faith and skill and care, there are a number of other duties imposed on a company (and thus on its directors). Below are examples of such duties which a director must consider.

Task:	Reference:	✍
1. Is the company trading fraudulently with the intent to defraud creditors or for any fraudulent purpose?	*Insolvency Act 1986, s 213*	☐
2. Is the company trading insolvently?	*Insolvency Act 1986, s 214*	☐
2.1 Have the directors concluded or ought they to conclude that there is no 'reasonable prospect' of the company avoiding insolvent liquidation?		☐
2.2 Has every step been taken with a view to minimising the loss to creditors?		☐
2.3 Would someone with the same general knowledge, skill and experience as the directors come to the same conclusion?		☐
3. If the company is insolvent, has any director retained, misapplied or become accountable for any property of the company, or been guilty of any misfeasance (wrongful exercise of authority)?	*Insolvency Act 1986, s 212*	☐

Practical Notes

The default of one director does not necessarily impose liability on the others.

Generally a director is under no duty to supervise the conduct of the other directors. However, there are exceptions to this rule, for example, the Takeover Panel has stressed the responsibility of the full board for the conduct of arrangements for a takeover offer.

There are numerous, miscellaneous, offences a director may potentially commit (e.g. in respect of the allotment of shares, without the authority required pursuant to section 80 of the Companies Act 1985; similarly directors will be personally liable to compensate any person who subscribes for shares or debentures in a company in reliance on untrue or misleading statements contained in a prospectus issued by a company).

There are also many instances where a director may commit a criminal offence in the course of the administration of the company, as detailed in Schedule 24 of the Companies Act 1985. Some of these offences are relatively trivial but, the court can impose penalties ranging from fairly small fines following summary conviction (in a Magistrates Court) to imprisonment and unlimited fines on conviction on indictment (in a Crown Court). The usual penalty imposed by the Companies Act 1985, however, for duties such as the filing of an annual return (CA 1985, s 363) is a default fine. It is usually the company secretary who will be responsible for such matters so it is important that the directors ensure that the secretary is competent and reliable and able to discharge these duties (see Checklist 1.3).

Some of the more serious offences (mostly involving fraud or dishonesty) carry severe penalties. For example, a director who publishes a written statement about the company which s/he knows is misleading, false or deceptive with intent to deceive the company's members or creditors about its affairs, may be sentenced to a term of 7 years imprisonment. In the case of offences not involving fraud or loss to others, the Department of Trade and Industry (which is responsible for enforcing company law) has tended not to bring prosecutions except where there has been a flagrant or persistent breach.

The directors are also responsible for monitoring the accounting records of the company and for producing appropriate profit and loss accounts and balance sheets in respect of each financial period, together with the directors' report (CA 1985, s 226).

6.3   Meetings of the Directors

Meetings of the directors (usually known as board meetings) are the normal forum for the directors to make decisions in relation to transacting the business of the company.

The proceedings of such meetings are usually regulated by a company's Articles of Association (see Checklist 2.3). Notwithstanding this, there are some general rules which do apply.

Company Secretary's Handbook reference: CSH 6.14

When preparing for a meeting of the directors the following checklist should be considered.

Fiduciary Duties

Company Secretary's Handbook reference: CSH 6.24

A director should be asking him/herself the following in respect of fiduciary duties.

Task:	Reference:	✍
1. Have all the directors been notified of the meeting in the usual way with reasonable notice and/or in accordance with any provision in the Articles of Association?	**Checklist 2.3** **CSH 6.18**	☐
2. Have all the directors received the agenda and board papers?	**CSH 6.18**	☐
3. If any of the directors are not in the UK, do the Articles of Association provide for these directors to receive notice of meetings?	**Checklist 2.3**	☐
4. Does the number of directors present at the meeting constitute a quorum under the Articles of Association?	**Checklist 2.3** **CSH 6.19**	☐
5. Has the process for decision making at directors' meetings as set out in the Articles of Association been followed?	**Checklist 2.3** **CSH 6.20**	☐
6. Has a copy of the minutes of the meeting of the board of directors signed by the chairman of the meeting been placed with the minutes of the previous meetings of the directors?	*CA 1985, s 382* **Checklist 3.6** **CSH 6.21**	☐

Practical Notes

A quorum is the minimum number of directors who must be present and entitled to participate in the meeting in order for the meeting to transact business.

If there is no reference to a matter in the minutes of meeting, case law has shown this to be prima facia proof that it has not been brought before the company. It is therefore important that appropriate minutes of the meetings of the directors are maintained.

Articles of Association will often provide for directors to be in attendance at meetings by telephone (CSH 6.22).

Most Articles of Association:

- *allow for the directors to pass resolutions in writing (CA 1985, Table A, Reg 93);*

- *allow for a director to appoint an alternate director if they are unable to attend a meeting (CA 1985, Table A, Regs 65–69);*
- *provide that if a director does not attend board meetings on six consecutive occasions he will automatically vacate office as a director (see Checklist 6.4) (CA 1985, Table A, Reg 81(e)); and*
- *allow for the directors to appoint a chairman from amongst themselves and for this individual to have a second and casting vote (CA 1985, Table A, Reg 88).*

The Combined Code, which is best practice for companies subject to the UK Listing Authority's Listing Rules, requires companies to have a list of matters reserved for the decision of the directors.

There are many other matters that also usually need the approval of the board of directors, for instance, the approval of transfers of shares, the convening of shareholders' meetings and the approval of documents requiring execution under the company seal or on behalf of the company.

The frequency of directors' meetings will usually depend on the company.

For most companies there is no prescribed length of notice for board meetings, although the courts have held that 'reasonable' notice should be given.

A sole director, if the Articles of Association of the company provide for him/her to act on his own, will usually merely resolve decisions, as a discussion is clearly not possible.

Minutes of a meeting of the board of directors signed by the chairman of that meeting are evidence of the decisions made unless the contrary is proved by, for example, the Court establishing they contained inaccuracies (CA 1985, s 382).

6.4   **Removal of a Director**

Section 303 of the *Companies Act 1985* deals with the removal of directors and gives the members of a company the ability to remove a director, which is a provision a company cannot exclude in its Articles of Association. In practice, however, this provision is rarely used. Rather, most directors are either asked by the company to resign or the Articles of Association of a company will often provide other mechanisms for the removal of directors (for instance, by allowing for the removal of a director by the approval of a majority of the other directors). As *CA 1985, s 303* requires special notice to be given to remove a director, it is usually quicker to amend a company's Articles so as to include such a mechanism.

The following are the issues to consider when removing a director.

Task:	**Reference:**	✍
1. Are you sure that the director cannot be persuaded to resign?		☐
2. Have you checked the Articles to see if there are any provisions that allow for the removal of a director by the shareholders or the other directors? If so:	*CA 1985, s 288* **Checklists 2.3, 3.2**	☐
2.1 follow the procedure set out in the Articles;		☐
2.2 obtain the necessary consents to effect the removal of the director;		☐
2.3 file Form 288b at Companies House; and		☐
2.4 update the register of directors.		☐

Only if the answers to the above are negative will you need to consider the following points.

3. If you cannot obtain such consents, can you pass a special resolution to amend the Articles so that you can remove the director?	**Checklists 2.3, 7.1**	☐
4. If the director has habitually not attended board meetings, do the Articles provide for his removal?	**Checklist 2.3**	☐
5. Does the director's service contract provide for his removal as a director?		☐
6. Is the director due to retire by rotation at an annual general meeting in the near future?	**Checklist 7.5**	☐
7. Has an officer served special notice on the company in respect of the proposed removal of the director?	*CA 1985, s 303(2)* **Checklist 7.11**	☐
8. Has the director been notified of the proposed resolution to remove them as a director?	*CA 1985, s 304(1)*	☐
9. Have you followed the procedure for an extraordinary general meeting?	**Checklist 7.2**	☐

10. Has the director made a written representation to the company?   *CA 1985, s 304(2)* ☐
    If so, has this been circulated to all the members of the company
    and does the notice of the extraordinary general meeting note
    that such a representation has been made?

11. Following the passing of the resolution, has Companies House   *CA 1985, s 288* ☐
    been notified of the removal by way of Form 288b?   **Checklist 5.1**

12. Has the register of directors been updated?   **Checklist 3.2** ☐

Practical Notes

A resolution proposed pursuant to CA 1985, s 303 cannot be passed as a written resolution but will need to be passed at a meeting of the members of the company.

Directors will often also be employees of the company. The cessation of an individual as an employee, however, is a separate matter which will need to be dealt with appropriately (e.g. in accordance with the terms of his/her service agreement) and, in relation to which, professional assistance may be required.

If the director can be persuaded to resign then the secretary should obtain a letter of resignation from the director, update the register of directors (see Checklist 3.2) and notify Companies House (using Form 288b) of the resignation. The resignation of the director should also be noted at the next board meeting of the company.

6.5   Loans to Directors

The general rule is that a company cannot make loans to directors. Any loans made by a company in contravention of *section 330* of the *Companies Act 1985* are voidable and the director in question could be liable to make good any loss for which repayment is not obtained from a third party and to account for his own profit (*CA1985, s 341*). In addition the directors of a company which authorises or permits the company to enter into such an arrangement knowing or having reasonable cause to believe that the company was contravening *CA 1985, s 330* are guilty of a criminal offence (*CA 1985, s 342 (1)*).

Notwithstanding this, in certain circumstances, a company may make a loan to a director (*CA 1985, s 330(2)*) and set out below are examples of when this can be done.

Task:	**Reference:**	✍
1. Is the loan a quasi-loan to a director of the relevant company or its holding company not exceeding £5,000 in total and do the terms of the loan provide for repayment within two months of the loan being made?	*CA 1985, s 332(1)* **CSH 6.30**	☐
2. Is the loan to a director of the company or its holding company not exceeding a total of £5,000?	*CA 1985, s 334*	☐
3. Is the loan a transaction not exceeding a total of £10,000 entered into for a director by a relevant company in the ordinary course of business and on terms no more favourable than for any unconnected person?	*CA 1985, s 335(1)*	☐
4. Is the loan for expenditure incurred, or to be incurred, by a director in performance of his/her duties as an officer of the company, subject to such expenditure being approved by the members of the company in general meeting and, in the case of a relevant company, not exceeding a total of £20,000?	*CA 1985, s 337(3)*	☐
5. Where the ordinary business of the company includes the making of loans or quasi-loans, is the loan or quasi-loan to a director of the company or its holding company, not exceeding a total of £100,000 (in the case of a relevant company), made in the ordinary course of business and on terms no more favourable than for any unconnected person of the same financial standing?	*CA 1985, s 338(4)*	☐

Practical Notes

For these purposes:

- *a **relevant company** is:*
  - *(a) a public limited company; or*
  - *(b) a subsidiary of a public limited company; or*
  - *(c) a subsidiary of a company which has as another subsidiary a public company; or*
  - *(d) a subsidiary which is a public company; and*
- *a **quasi-loan** is a transaction under which the company agrees to pay, or pays otherwise than in pursuance of an agreement, a sum for a director or agrees to reimburse, or reimburse otherwise than in pursuance of an agreement, expenditure incurred by another party for the director.*

These restrictions also apply to:

- *persons connected with a director, such as a spouse or minor child (CA 1985, s 346);*
- *any company in which a director is interested in at least one-fifth of the equity share capital; and*
- *any company in which a director can control the exercise of more than one-fifth of the votes.*

135

6.6   Directors' Interests

In broad terms in this context, the term 'directors' interests' refers to any shares or options which an individual holds in a company of which he is a director (*CA 1985, s 324*).

The general position is that a director has a duty to disclose his/her interests in shares in the company and a company must maintain a register of directors' interests. However, a company is also obliged to include in the register of directors' interests details of, for example, any grants of share options to directors (*CA 1985, s 325(3)*).

Schedule 13 of the *Companies Act 1985* sets out the precise nature of such interests that need to be disclosed (and thus registered). Unfortunately, this is one of the more complex areas of the *Companies Act 1985* and it is, therefore, not possible to include a complete list of interests that would need to be disclosed within the confines of this book. As an alternative, therefore, we have detailed some useful examples of interests that must be disclosed (see also Checklist 3.3).

Company Secretary's Handbook reference: CSH 3.1

When judging whether a director has an interest pursuant to *CA 1985, s 324* the following should be considered.

Task:		Reference:	✍
1.	Is s/he a beneficiary of a trust, the property of which includes any interests in shares, options or debentures of the company?	*CA 1985, Sch 13, para 2*	☐
2.	Does a body corporate own the shares or debentures and the body corporate is accustomed to acting in accordance with the directions of the director in question, or does such director own one third of the voting rights of the body corporate?	*CA 1985, Sch 13, para 4*	☐
3.	Has s/he entered into a contract to purchase shares in the capital of the company?	*CA 1985, Sch 13, para 3(1)*	☐
4.	Has s/he the right (exercisable presently or in the future) to call for the delivery of shares to him/her or at his/her order?	*CA 1985, Sch 13, para 6(2)*	☐
5.	Is s/he entitled to exercise any rights in those shares or debentures (except rights of proxy or in his/her role as a company representative?	*CA 1985, Sch 13, para 3(1)*	☐
6.	Are the spouse or minor offspring (under 18) of the director interested?	*CA 1985, s 328*	☐

Practical Notes

There are a number of interests that do not need to be notified, such as where the director is acting as a bare trustee or in respect of unit trusts. If you are unsure, you will need to look at Schedule 13 of the Companies Act 1985 with some care.

A director is also obliged to notify the company of his/her interests in a company's holding company or subsidiary (CA 1985, s 324).

Directors are obliged to notify the company in writing both when they become and when they cease to be interested in shares, when they enter into a contract to sell any shares in which they are interested or to assign any right granted to them by the company to subscribe for shares (CA 1985, s 324(2)).

A company is obliged to maintain a register of directors' interests (CA 1985, s 325(1)) (see Checklist 3.3).

The secretary should, on a regular basis, remind directors generally of their obligations in this regard and especially if s/he becomes aware of some event that leads him/her to believe that a notification or amendment to the register needs to be made. The penalties in respect of directors' interests in shares are, theoretically at least, some of the most stringent (CA 1985, Sch 24).

Since a company's annual accounts will include details of directors' interests, any discrepancies in the register of directors' interests will be highlighted by disclosures made in the accounts.

Where a listed company receives a notification of a director's interest, it must notify the appropriate regulatory exchange of such interest, without delay, which may then publish the information.

7 Membership

Contents

7.1   Resolutions

The members of a company will on different occasions need to resolve to carry out certain acts. Resolutions are required to effect various changes or actions of the company. The *Companies Act 1985* provides for a number of different resolutions. These are, for example as follows.

Type of resolution	Examples of where used
Ordinary **CSH 7.58**	Increase authorised share capital *CA 1985, s 123* Checklist 8.1 Authorisation of directors to allot shares *CA 1985, s 80(8)* Checklist 8.11 Removal of director *CA 1985, s 303* Checklist 6.4 Resolution to re-appoint auditor at an annual general meeting *CA 1985, ss 385, 385A* Checklist 7.5
Extraordinary **CSH 7.59**	Members voluntary liquidation *Insolvency Act 1986, s 84(1)(c)* Class meeting to sanction a variation of rights *CA 1985, s 125(2)(b)* Checklist 8.17
Special **CSH 7.60**	Change of name *CA 1985, s 28* Checklist 2.8 Change of Articles of Association *CA 1985, s 9* Checklist 2.3 Alteration of the objects *CA 1985, s 4* Checklist 2.1 Re-registrations Checklists 2.9-2.12 Purchase of own shares *CA 1985, ss 164, 155* Checklist 8.6-8.9 Disapplication of pre-emption rights *CA 1985, s 95* Checklist 8.11

Elective **CSH 7.61**	To dispense with requirements to hold an annual general meeting, to lay accounts and reports before the company in general meeting, and to appoint auditors annually *CA 1985, ss 252 366A, 386* Checklist 7.7
Written **CSH 7.63**	Anything which may be done by resolution of a private limited company but *not the removal of a director or an auditor.* *CA 1985, s 381A* Checklists 4.18, 6.4

Requirements for Different Resolutions

As mentioned in a number of the checklists, different actions of the companies require different types of resolutions and these resolutions have a variety of requirements. For example, some resolutions require specific details to be given. The following table summarises the requirements.

Type of resolution	Specify in Notice	Minimum notice period (clear days)	Voting Majority	Filing with Registrar
Ordinary	Not required	14 days	Simple majority of votes cast	Depends on the type of resolution
Extraordinary	Yes	14 days	Three quarters of votes cast	Always
Special	Yes	21 days	Three quarters of votes cast	Always
Elective	Yes	21 days	All votes capable of being cast to be cast in favour	Always

Practical Notes

If the Companies Act 1985 and the Articles of Association of the company do not require a particular resolution, an ordinary resolution will suffice. Section 380 of the Companies Act 1985 sets out the general requirement for filing resolutions at Companies House.

By 'Specify in notice', we mean give specific details of the proposed resolution in the notice convening the general meeting (see Checklist 7.2).

When issuing a notice of general meeting, the Articles of Association should be checked to see whether 'clear days' is defined. To be prudent, the date of service of the notice should be excluded, as should the date of the meeting. Many Articles of Association deem that the notice is served 48 hours after posting.

Ordinary resolutions that need to be filed at Companies House are, for example, a resolution to increase capital pursuant to section 123 of the Companies Act 1985 (see Checklist 8.1) or a resolution passed pursuant to section 80 of the Companies Act 1985 to authorise the directors to issue shares (see Checklist 8.11).

Section 378 of the Companies Act 1985 sets out the necessary majorities for the company to pass special and extraordinary resolutions.

The date on which a resolution is passed is the date of the meeting where it was approved either by a general meeting or in writing or, if the resolution was passed at an adjourned meeting, the date of the adjourned meeting (CA 1985, s 381) (see Checklist 7.2).

A written resolution can be used to replace a special, extraordinary or elective resolution. Voting majorities do not apply to written resolutions as unanimity is required (see Checklist 7.10).

See also Checklist 7.5.

7.2   General Meetings

General meetings of the members of a company are either extraordinary general meetings or annual general meetings. An extraordinary general meeting is any meeting other than an annual general meeting (which means that they are not extraordinary at all!). However, the popularity of companies passing resolutions as written resolutions has meant that amongst private companies they have become less common. Extraordinary general meetings should be called when there is urgent business that cannot be left to the next annual general meeting (Checklist 7.5).

It is not possible within this book to provide a checklist dealing with all matters but the following should be considered when convening an general meeting.

Before the Meeting:

Task:		Reference:	✍
1.	Have you considered whether the proposed resolution would be better passed as a written resolution?	*CA 1985, s 381A* **Checklist 7.10**	☐
2.	Has the venue for the proposed meeting been booked and correctly described in the notice?		☐
3.	Is the venue appropriate for anticipated attendance, given previous experience and anticipated shareholder and publicity interest this year?		☐
4.	Have the auditors been informed of the proposed general meeting date and venue?	*CA 1985, ss 370(2), 390(1)*	☐
5.	Have you checked the quorum provisions for general meetings contained in the Articles of Association and considered whether it is likely there will be a quorum of members present at the meeting?	**Checklist 2.3**	☐
6.	Have you checked that the directors have the power to call a general meeting?	*CA 1985, Table A, Reg 37* **Checklist 2.3**	☐
7.	Has a script for the Chairman been prepared including a poll procedure?	**Checklist 7.9**	☐

Notice of Meeting:

8.	Is the notice dated and does it state the time, date and place for the meeting and the registered office of the company?	*CA 1985, Table A, Reg 38* **CSH 7.35–7.36**	☐
9.	Is there a statement of the rights of the shareholders to appoint proxies?	*CA 1985, s 372(3)* **CSH 7.25, Precedent C, Appendix 7B Checklist 7.8**	☐
10.	Has the notice period been checked, particularly against provisions in the Articles relating to service?	*CA 1985, s 369* **Checklists 2.3, 7.1**	☐

11.	Has the notice been approved by the board of directors and does it state that it is issued 'By Order of the Board', with the secretary's name?	*CA 1985, ss 368, 378(2)* ☐
12.	Have you considered whether it would be possible to obtain consent from the members for the meeting to be held at short notice?	*CA 1985, ss 369(3)(a), 378(3)* **CSH 7.36, Appendix 7B, Precedents E1, E2 Checklist 7.7** ☐
13.	Does the notice specify the nature of the business to be transacted at the meeting including specific details on certain resolutions?	**Checklist 7.1** ☐
14.	Has the notice been served on all those entitled to receive notice pursuant to the Articles of Association?	*CA 1985, s 370* **Checklist 2.3** ☐

After the meeting

15.	Following the meeting have the minutes of the meeting been signed by the Chairman and placed with the minute book?	**Checklist 3.6** ☐
16.	Once the meeting has been completed, do any of the resolutions need to be filed at Companies House and are any forms required e.g. a form 123 for an increase in share capital?	**Checklist 5.1** ☐

Practical Notes

In terms of preparation similar rules apply for an extraordinary general meeting as an annual general meeting (see Checklist 7.5).

Though it is not essential that all the directors are able to attend the extraordinary general meeting for practical reasons you need to ensure that the appropriate directors can attend the meeting.

The Articles of Association usually allow for the directors to call a general meeting (CA 1985, Table A, Reg 37).

Additional requirements are imposed for companies subject to the UK Listing Authority's Listing Rules.

The Companies Act 1985 (Electronic Communications) Order 2000 (SI 2000/3373) amended CA 1985 to specifically allow companies to sent out notice of meetings electronically to those entitled to receive them.

7.3 Requisitioning a Meeting of the Members of the Company

This is an extreme measure and only used when reason has failed to persuade a company to consider an issue of concern to a member. It is used to insist that the company calls an extraordinary general meeting.

A general meeting that is not specified in the notice of the meeting as being an annual general meeting is usually deemed to be a extraordinary general meeting (*CA 1985, Table A, Reg 36*) (see Checklist 7.2).

When a company receives a requisition of a meeting of the members they should consider the following checklist.

Task:	Reference:	✎
1. Do the members hold a tenth or more of the paid-up share capital carrying voting rights?	*CA 1985, s 368(2)* **CSH 7.49**	☐
2. Has the requisition, signed by all the requisitionists, been deposited at the registered office of the company?	*CA 1985, s 368(3)* **CSH 7.49**	☐
3. Does the requisition state the objects of the meeting?	*CA 1985, s 368(3)*	☐
4. Have you checked the Articles of Association for any unusual provision in respect of the requisition of a meeting of the members?		☐
4. Have the directors called an extraordinary general meeting within 21 days?	*CA 1985, s 368(4)* **Checklist 7.2**	☐
5. Is the notice of the meeting in order and does it convene a meeting not more than 28 days after the date of the notice?	*CA 1985, s 368(8)* **Checklist 7.2**	☐

Practical Notes

The most common reason for requisitioning a meeting is to remove a director but there are no limits to the business that such a meeting may be requisition for. A resigning auditor may also requisition a meeting (Checklist 4.9).

The directors usually have power to call a general meeting at any time (CA 1985, Table A, Reg 36).

If the directors do not convene an extraordinary general meeting the requisitionists may convene the meeting within three months (CA 1985, s 368(4)).

The company has additional duties pursuant to section 376 of the Companies Act 1985 on receiving a requisition in writing from:

- *one-twentieth of the total voting rights of all the members (CA 1985, s 376(2)(a)); or*
- *one hundred members holding shares in the company with an average paid up sum of not less than £100. (CA 1985, s 376(2)(b).)*
  Having received a requisition pursuant to section CA 1985, s 376(2) the company must circulate to the members at the members expense:
- *notice of any resolution which may be properly moved and is intended to be moved at that meeting (CA 1985, s 376(1)(a)); and*
- *any statement of not more than 1,000 words with respect to the meeting to be referred to in any roposed resolution or the business to be dealt with at that meeting (CA 1985, s 376(1)(b)).*

A copy of the requisition must be deposited at the registered office of the company:

- *not less that six weeks before the meeting where it requires notice of a resolution (CA 1985, s 377(1)(a)); or*
- *otherwise a week before the meeting (CA 1985, s 377(1)(b)).*

The requisitionists need to deposit with the company a reasonable sum to cover expenses.

7.4   Annual General Meetings

A company is required to have an annual meeting of members unless it has adopted the elective regime (see Checklist 7.7).

The business to be transacted at the annual general meeting (AGM) for each company will vary. The Articles of Association of the company should be checked to ensure all relevant requirements are satisfied.

This checklist needs to be read in conjunction with Checklists 7.2 and 7.5.

'Listed Company' in this context means a company subject to the Listing Rules of the UK Listing Authority.

Company Secretary's Handbook reference: CSH 7.41, App 7B

When proposing to convene an AGM, the following checklist should be considered.

The Notice – The Basics:

Task:	Reference:	✍
1. Is the AGM to be held within 15 months of the previous AGM and in successive calendar years, or within 18 months of incorporation?	*CA 1985, ss 366(1), (3)*	☐
2. Have you considered all those matters in the Checklist on general meetings – before the meeting and notice of meeting?	**Checklist 7.2**	☐
3. Have you considered Checklist 7.5?	**Checklist 7.5**	☐
4. Have you considered where special notice is required for any of the proposed resolutions?	**Checklist 7.11**	☐

The Notice – The Basics for Listed Companies:

5. Will the registrars be required to close the register, provide address labels for the posting of the notice or attend the AGM?		☐
6. Is the notice to be sent at least 20 working days before the meeting?	**CC para C.2.4**	☐
7. Has first class post for shareholders in Member States (and air mail for others) been arranged?	**LR 9.29-9.30**	☐
8. For companies in CREST, does the notice set out the cut off times for recognising changes in the register of members for voting purposes, and more than 48 hours before the meeting?	**Uncertificated Securities Regulations 1995 (SI 1995/3272), Reg 41**	☐
9. Does the explanatory circular need to be submitted to the UK Listing Authority and does it comply with the general requirements for circulars?	**LR 14.1, 14.17-14.19**	☐
10. Is the AGM to be invited to approve the company's policy on remuneration?	**CC para B.3.5**	☐

11. Will the chairman of the audit, nomination and remuneration committees be available to answer questions at the AGM?   **CC para C.2.3**   ☐

12. Have you included an appropriate proxy card?   **Checklist 7.8**   ☐

13. Have two copies of the notice been lodged with the UK Listing Authority?   **LR 9.31, 14.4**   ☐

After the Notice has been Posted – The Basics:

14. Have you the necessary documents for display at the annual general meeting?   **Checklist 7.6**   ☐

15. Following the meeting have the minutes of meeting been signed by the Chairman and placed with the minute book?   **Checklist 3.6**   ☐

16. Do any of the resolutions passed at the meeting need to be notified to Companies House and are any statutory forms required e.g. Form 123 for an increase in share capital?   **Checklist 5.1**   ☐

After the Notice has been Posted – The Basics for Listed Companies

17. Is the market aware of the time and date of the meeting?   ☐

18. Have you made provision for any proposed trading statement to be made to the market simultaneously with release to the meeting?   **LR 9.1**   ☐

19. Have you forwarded copies of the resolutions to the UK Listing Authority of any matter other than ordinary business?   **LR 9.31(b)**   ☐

Practical Notes

The register of members of listed companies is usually maintained by a registrar.

If the intention is to hold the annual general meeting at less than the usual notice, the consent of all the members needs to be obtained.

Clear days excludes the date of issue and receipt of the notice. The Articles of Association should be checked to see whether receipt is deemed to be, for example, the day after posting or two days (see Checklist 2.3).

7.5 Resolutions Commonly Included in the Notice of Annual General Meetings

This is a checklist for a listed company subject to the UK Listing Authority's Listing Rules. However it contains much which is best practice for all companies that are required to have an annual general meeting (see Checklists 7.4, 7.6).

Private limited companies will normally only pass the resolutions listed in 4.1, 4.2, 4.3, 4.4 and 4.5 below. Private companies will not normally seek an authority for the directors to issue shares as most will probably have a more enduring power already in place (Checklist 8.11). As so many private companies have adopted the elective regime it is becoming far less usual for them to hold annual general meetings (see Checklist 7.7).

Company Secretary's Handbook reference: CSH 7.42.

When preparing the notice of annual general meeting for a listed company, subject to the UK Listing Authority's Listing Rules, have you considered the following checklist?

The Notice – The Basics:

Task:	Reference:	✍
1. Does the notice contain separate resolutions on each substantially separate issue?	**CC para C.2.2**	☐
2. Do the Articles of Association have any requirements relating to special business or other specific resolutions and have such requirements been satisfied?	**Checklist 2.3**	☐
3. Is there an explanation of any special business proposed at the annual general meeting, either in a separate circular or in the directors' report?	**LR 14.17**	☐

Ordinary Resolutions

4. Does the notice contain details of the ordinary resolutions to be proposed at the annual general meeting:	*CA 1985, ss 80, 241, 385(2), 390A(1)* **CC paras A.6.2, C.2.2 LR 14.7 Association of British Insurers (ABI) Guidelines**	☐
4.1 to receive, consider and approve the accounts and the reports of the directors and the auditors on the accounts;		☐
4.2 to declare the final dividend if the company is proposing to declare a final dividend;		☐
4.3 to elect directors appointed since the last general meeting;		☐
4.4 to re-elect directors retiring by rotation;		☐

4.5   to re-appoint the auditors and/or authorise the directors to fix their remuneration and, if the auditors have changed, is special notice required; and ☐

4.6   to give the directors authority to allot shares? ☐

5.   Have you: *CA 1985, ss 292, 293,* ☐
                                                                                     385(2), 390A(1)
    CC para A.6.2
    Checklists 2.3, 4.17

5.1   checked the Articles to see if directors are required to retire by rotation and if so the order of directors retiring by rotation; ☐

5.2   checked that all directors have been subject to re-election of intervals of no more than three years if required to rotate pursuant to the Articles; ☐

5.3   checked the Articles to see if directors appointed since the last annual general meeting are required to be elected at the next general meeting? ☐

5.4   ensured that appointments are voted on individually; ☐

5.5   noted any special requirements applicable to directors over the retirement age (which is 70 unless varied by the Articles); and ☐

5.6   decided to re-appoint the auditors and authorise the directors to fix their remuneration (check need for special notice if auditors changed)? ☐

6.   Does the circular or statement in the directors' report relating to the directors' authority to allot shares: *CA 1985, s 80(4)* ☐
    LR 14.7
    ABI Guidelines

6.1   detail the maximum amount of shares covered by the authority and the percentage which that amount represents of the total issued ordinary share capital at a date not more than one month prior to the date of the circular or report; ☐

6.2   include a statement as to whether the directors presently intend to exercise the authority and, if so, for what purpose; ☐

6.3   state the expiry date of the authority which needs to be a specific date of a period of not more than five years (but best practice would be to seek authorisation every year at each annual general meeting); and ☐

6.4   have the maximum amount of the authority as the *lesser* of: ☐

6.4.1   the unissued equity share capital; and ☐

6.4.2 one third of the issued equity share capital *plus* amounts for which the company requires an additional specific power under *CA 1985, s 80* (e.g. to satisfy the company's obligations to issue shares in respect of deferred consideration or options)? ☐

Special Resolutions Often Included in the Notice of an Annual General Meeting of a Listed Company

7.   Is there a resolution in respect of the disapplication of pre-emption rights on equity issued for cash, and if so does the circular or statement in the directors' report: **LR 14.8(a), (b)**
ABI Guidelines ☐

   7.1   have a statement of: ☐

      7.1.1   the maximum amount of shares which the disapplication will cover, and ☐

      7.1.2   in the case of a general disapplication, the percentage which the disapplied amount represents of the total issued ordinary share capital as at a date not more than one month prior to the date of the circular or report; and ☐

   7.2   have the maximum amount of authority as 5% of the issued ordinary share capital or 7.5% in any three year period? ☐

8.   Is there a resolution in respect of the authority to purchase own shares and, if so, does the circular or statement in the directors' report: *CA 1985, ss 89-96, 162, 166(4)*
LR 15.4(a)-(f)
ABI Guidelines ☐

   8.1   disapply statutory pre-emption rights on equity issues for cash? ☐

   8.2   give the authority to purchase its own shares? ☐

   8.3   in the case of a general authority, state the directors' intentions for using the authority sought; ☐

   8.4   include, if known, the number of shares to be acquired and the method of acquisition; ☐

   8.5   include details of specific purchases proposed; ☐

   8.6   include details of the price, or the maximum and minimum price, to be paid; ☐

   8.7   include details of the total numbers of warrants and options to subscribe for equity shares that are outstanding and the proportion of issued share capital ☐

that they represent both before and after the buy-back authority being sought is used in full;

8.8 include other required information as required by LR 14.1; ☐

8.9 limit the authority to 10% of issued ordinary share capital; and ☐

8.10 state that the maximum duration of authority is eighteen months (good practice is fifteen months, although the ABI requires the authority to be renewed annually)? ☐

Practical Notes

The Companies Act 1985 (Electronic Communications) Order 2000 (SI 2000/3373) made under Section 8 of the Electronic Communications Act 2000, came into effect on 22 December 2000. The order allows companies to send Companies Act 1985 documents (e.g. annual report and accounts, notice of annual general meeting) to a member electronically where the member agrees. It also enables companies, where a member agrees, to place a document on a website and to send the member a notice of availability of the document in lieu of sending the document itself. The Institute of Chartered Secretaries & Administrators has published a best practice guide called 'Electronic Communications with Shareholders'.

Chapter 15 of the UK Listing Authority Listing Rules sets out other requirements in relation to purchase of own shares. In particular, if a listed company wishes to acquire its own shares which are not equity shares, see LR 15.13 to 15.18.

For AIM companies, for instance, three copies of all documents sent to the shareholders need to be sent to the London Stock Exchange.

7.6   Documents to be Displayed at the AGM

The following is a list of documents that you will need to display at the Annual General Meeting of a company subject to the UK Listing Authority Listing Rules.

The Notice – The Basics:

Task:	Reference:	✍
1. Register of Members.		☐
2. Signed copy of the Annual Report and Accounts for members to take away.		☐
3. Directors' service contracts.	**LR 16.9(b)**	☐
4. Register of Directors' Interests.	*CA 1985, s 325(5), Schedule 13, Part IV, para 29*	☐
5. Details of all proxies received.	**CC para C.2.1**	☐
6. Memorandum and Articles of Association.		☐

Practical Notes

Companies that are not subject to the UK Listing Authority's Listing Rules will not need to include the directors' service contracts or details of all proxies received.

7.7 Elective Resolutions

Private companies may now elect to reduce certain obligations under the *Companies Act 1985*. The most common is to elect not to hold an annual meeting of shareholders as such a meeting would be a formality.

As part of the Department of Trade and Industry review of company law, the Final Report of the Company Law Review Steering Group proposed that private companies will automatically be exempt from holding annual general meetings unless the company resolves otherwise.

Company Secretary's Handbook reference: CSH 7.61.

When dealing with elective resolutions, company secretaries should consider the following checklist.

Task:	Reference:	✍
1. Has the private company elected not to hold an annual meeting of the members by dispensing with certain obligations, such as:	*CA 1985, ss 252, 366A(1), 379A, 386(1)* **CSH 4.49, Precedents H, J, K, Appendix 7B**	☐
1.1 the obligation to lay accounts before members annually;		☐
1.2 the requirement to hold an annual general meeting; or		☐
1.3 the annual appointment of auditors?		☐
2. Additionally, has the private company elected to take advantage of certain other concessions, for example:	*CA 1985, ss 80A, 369* **CSH Precedents G, L, Appendix 7B**	☐
2.1 directors may be authorised to allot shares pursuant to *section 80* of the *Companies Act 1985* for an indefinite period in excess of five years; and		☐
2.2 the company may reduce the majority required for short notice from 95 per cent of the members entitled to attend and vote to 90 per cent?		☐

Most private companies should adopt the first three exemptions as annual meetings of the members are a formality. Few companies elect to reduce the majority needed for consents to short notice or to extend the period for which the directors are authorised to allot shares (see Checklist 8.11).

A private company should consider the following when adopting the elective regime.

3. Has the adoption of the elective regime been approved unanimously by all the members entitled to attend and vote at a general meeting either at a general meeting or by a written resolution?	*CA 1985, s 379A(2)(b)* **Checklists 7.1, 7.2, 7.10**	☐
4. Has a copy of the elective resolution been filed at Companies House within 15 days of the passing of the resolution?	*CA 1985, s 380(1)* **Checklist 5.1**	☐

5.   If the elective regime is revoked has this been notified to   *CA 1985, s 380(1)*   ☐
Companies House within 15 days of the revocation?   **Checklist 5.1**

6.   If the company has elected not to hold an annual general   *CA 1985, s 253(1)*   ☐
meeting do all the accounts of the company following this
election state that there will be no annual general meeting unless
a request is received from either an auditor or member?

7.   Are all accounts posted to all the members at least 28 days   *CA 1985, s 253(1)*   ☐
before the time for filing the accounts with Companies House?

Practical Notes

Elective resolutions are normally adopted by written instrument (see Checklist 7.10).

Public companies may not adopt the elective regime and if a private company re-registers as a public company all elective resolutions cease to have effect (CA 1985, s 379A(4)).

An elective resolution in respect of the laying of accounts applies to the report and accounts for the year in which the election is made and cannot retrospectively apply to financial periods which have ended.

The members may by ordinary resolution revoke an elective resolution (CA 1985, s 379(3)).

If an auditor resigns while the elective regime is in force the directors may fill the casual vacancy (CA 1985, s 388(1)) (see Checklist 4.17).

7.8   Proxies

Proxies are used when a member is unable to attend a meeting.

Any member of a company entitled to attend and vote at a general meeting is entitled to appoint another person (whether a member or not) as a proxy to attend and vote on their behalf (*CA 1985, s 372(1)*). In the case of a company having a share capital, in every notice calling a meeting of the company there must appear a statement that a member who is entitled to attend and vote is entitled to appoint a proxy. The Articles of Association of many companies will set out a procedure for appointing proxies (*CA 1985, Table A, Reg 59-63*).

Further requirements are imposed on listed companies subject to the UK Listing Authority's Listing Rules. However private companies with a substantial number of members may find it helps their members if they provide a proxy card.

Members need to be treated in a uniform manner as the directors would commit an offence if they issued, for example, a proxy card to certain members only (*CA 1985, s 372(7)*).

Company Secretary's Handbook reference: CSH 7.28, Appendix 7B

For companies considering preparing a proxy card, in particular listed companies, the following checklist should be considered.

Task:	Reference:	✎
1. Will a proxy card be sent, with the notice convening a meeting, to each person entitled to vote at the meeting?	**LR 9.26, 13.28(a)**	☐
2. Does the proxy card:	*CA 1985, s 372(1)* **LR 13.28(b)-(d)**	☐
2.1 provide for two-way voting on all non-procedural resolutions;		☐
2.2 include language empowering the proxy to vote on 'any other business which may properly come before the meeting';		☐
2.3 include a statement that a member is entitled to appoint a proxy of his choice and provide a space for insertion of the name of such proxy;		☐
2.4 state that a proxy need not be a member;		☐
2.5 state that if the card is returned without an indication as to how the proxy should vote on any particular matter, the proxy will exercise his discretion as to whether, and how, he votes; and		☐
2.6 ask the member to sign the card?		
3. If the number of directors retiring and standing for re-election is more than five, does the proxy card allow the member to vote for or against their re-election as a whole, as well as individually?	**LR 13.29**	☐

4. Does it indicate the place and latest date and time for effective   *CA 1985, s 372(5)*   ☐
    lodgement and does this comply with the relevant provisions in
    the Articles?

5. Have two copies of the proxy card been lodged with the UK   **LR 13.1(f), 13.2**   ☐
    Listing Authority at the time of issue?

Practical Notes

For companies not subject to the UK Listing Authority Listing Rules only items 2.4 and 4 need to be complied with and a separate card would not be essential.

If a larger number of people are expected to attend the annual general meeting the proxy cards can be personalised by bar-coding.

Many listed companies use attendance cards to assist with the smooth running of the annual general meeting.

Most companies word the proxy card so that the chairman is appointed as a proxy unless a specific person is chosen.

Under the Companies Act 1985 (Electronic Communications) Order 2000 (SI 2000/3373), if a company so wishes, members will be able to transmit electronically to the company details of any proxy appointments, despite any provisions to the contrary in the Articles of Association.

The maximum time that a company can require that proxy forms are lodged with the company prior to the meeting is forty eight hours (CA 1985, s 372(5)).

There has been debate whether faxed proxy cards should be accepted. Practically many companies would accept a faxed proxy card.

If a member does attend and votes in person at a meeting this invalidates their proxy card.

A company may appoint a person to represent them at a general meeting of a company (CA 1985, s 375). A representative may exercise the same powers on behalf of shareholders as if they were an individual member.

7.9   Poll Procedure

A poll can be taken of the members of a company to decide issues at, for example, general meetings (see Checklist 7.2). A poll is a vote conducted by voting papers rather than a show of hands. It allows the number of shares that an individual holds to be taken into account rather than the single vote the member would get on a 'show of hands'. In most companies each member has one vote for each share which he holds on a poll (*CA 1985, Table A, Reg 54*). The Articles of Association of other companies often vary the voting rights of different classes of shares (see Checklist 8.17).

This is the procedure to use at a meeting of the members to assess the level of support when pursuant to the Articles of Association a poll is demanded.

Company Secretary's Handbook reference: CSH 7.32.

The following should be considered when a request for a poll is made at a general meeting.

Task:	Reference:	✍
1. Has the poll been validly called pursuant to the Articles of Association which, if the *CA 1985, Table A* is in force, it would be by:	**Checklist 2.3**	☐
1.1 the Chairman; or		☐
1.2 at least two members having the right to vote; or		☐
1.3 a member or members holding not less than one-tenth of the total voting shares; or		☐
1.4 a member or members holding shares conferring a right to vote at the meeting, being shares on which an aggregate sum has been paid up equal to not less than one-tenth of the total sum paid up on all the shares conferring that right?		☐
2. If the proxy vote is overwhelmingly either for or against the resolution has the chairman suggested to those demanding the poll that they withdraw the request?		☐
3. Has the chairman indicated the procedure to be followed in respect of the mechanics of the poll and whether the poll will be held immediately or at the end of the meeting and, at the appropriate time, outlined the procedure to follow?		☐
4. Has a scrutineer been appointed (often solicitors or auditors)?		☐
5. At the time of the poll has a steward distributed the poll card or ballot paper to all members present leaving a space for completion for:		☐
5.1 the name of the members (together with sufficient information to clearly identify the member);		☐
5.2 the number of shares being voted;		☐

5.3   an indication of which way the member is voting these shares on each resolution; and ☐

5.4   the member to sign the card? ☐

6.   Has the scrutineer: ☐

6.1   checked the poll cards or ballot papers; ☐

6.2   verified the holdings against the register of members; ☐

6.3   checked, where the vote is given by proxy, that the proxy holder has been properly appointed and the proxy holder has followed the members instructions (if any); ☐

6.4   eliminated any proxy vote where the member has voted in person; and ☐

6.5   prepared a report and final certificate of the result of the poll showing all votes for and against? ☐

7.   Has the chairman announced the result and in the case of a listed company made an appropriate announcement? ☐

Practical Notes

The chairman should call a poll if he is holding proxies which would reverse the decision of a vote on a show of hands.

Some listed companies now call a poll on all resolutions; the theory being that it allows all members to participate in the vote, not just those at the meeting.

It is generally preferable to hold the poll at the close of the meeting otherwise it can make the meeting quite disjointed.

Under CA 1985, s 373, any provision in the Articles is void which:

- *excludes the right to demand a poll at a general meeting on any question other than the election of the chairman of the meeting or the adjournment of the meeting; or*
- *makes ineffective a demand for a poll on any such question which is made either:*
    - *by not less than five members having the right to vote at the meeting;*
    - *by a member or members representing not less than one-tenth of the total voting rights of all the members having the right to vote at the meeting; or*
    - *by a member or members holding shares in the company conferring a right to vote at the meeting, being shares on which an aggregate sum has been paid up equal to not less than one tenth of the total sum paid up on all the shares conferring that right.*

Proxy holders have the right to demand a poll pursuant to Section 373(2) of the Companies Act 1985 (see Checklist 7.8).

On a poll taken at a meeting of a company or a meeting of any class of members of a company, a member entitled to more than one vote need not, if he votes, use all his votes or cast all the votes he uses in the same way (CA 1985, s 374). Similarly for large companies it is highly likely that a chairman would hold two proxies which vote in opposing directions.

Preparation for a poll needs to take place prior to the meeting. Proxies received need to be tabulated prior to the meeting. This will often give a guide as to the likelihood of the poll being called. Ideally the chairman should be provided with a poll script to ensure an appropriate procedure is followed. In addition, you need to decide who will be appointed scrutineers, ballot papers need to be produced and an up-to-date list of members must be available.

7.10   Written Resolutions

Most acts that require approval of the members of the company can be dealt with by written resolutions. Increasingly it is the favoured way of dealing with such matters as changes of name of private limited companies.

Written resolutions are not and should not be described as a specific type of resolution, but rather as an alternative manner of passing resolutions (see Checklist 7.1). It is probably not necessary to describe a resolution as anything other than a written resolution, but it is usual to differentiate between, for instance, special and ordinary resolutions by their headings.

The procedure for written resolutions for private companies is governed by *CA 1985, s 381* and overrides the provisions contained in the Memorandum and Articles of Association of the company (*CA 1985, s 381C*).

Company Secretary's Handbook reference: CSH 3.52.

When preparing a written resolution the following checklist should be considered.

Task:		Reference:	✍
1.	Does the written resolution include:	*CA 1985, s 381*	☐
	1.1 the full name of the company;		☐
	1.2 the company number;		☐
	1.3 the date of each person signing the resolution; and		☐
	1.4 the fact that it has been executed by all the members?		☐
2.	If the company has an auditor have they been sent a copy of the resolution?	*CA 1985, s 381B*	☐
3.	Have all the members entitled to attend and vote at a general meeting of the company signed the resolution?	*CA 1985, s 381A(1)*	☐
4.	Has the resolution been filed at Companies House, as it would have been required had it been passed at a general meeting?	*CA 1985, s 381A(6)* **Checklist 5.1**	☐
5.	Does the written resolution state that it is either passed:		☐
	5.1 pursuant to *CA 1985, s 381A* (private companies only); or		☐
	5.2 pursuant to the Articles of Association?		☐
6.	Has the written resolution been recorded in the minute book?	**Checklist 3.6**	☐

Practical Notes

The Articles of Association of most companies allow them to pass resolutions in writing and are used by public limited companies to pass written resolutions (CA 1985, Table A, Reg 53).

Written resolutions may not be used to remove either directors and auditors (see Checklists 4.18, 6.4) (CA 1985, Sch 15A(1)). The procedural requirements for written resolutions are varied in the case of a few specific resolutions, for example, the approval of the payment out of capital (CA 1985, Sch 15A) (see Checklist 8.7).

Generally, a written resolution must be signed by all members holding shares that could vote on the resolution in general meeting. All joint holders of a voting share must sign unless the Articles authorise one of them as a sole person entitled to vote the shares on behalf of the others. If CA 1985, Table A applies to the company without modification all members must sign.

If a member is not eligible to vote on a matter pursuant to the Articles of Association, they are similarly not eligible to sign the written resolution in the same manner but would not effect the validity of the written resolution.

A written resolution becomes effective at the time the last member signs the resolution (CA 1985, s 381A(3)). Companies House insist that written resolutions are dated.

When notifying the auditors of the written resolution it is a good idea to do so by fax so that you have a receipt.

The signatures of the members do not have to appear on the same resolution provided all the signed resolutions are in the same form (CA 1985, s 381A(2)).

If documents are required to be circulated to members with a notice of general meeting or made available at the registered office of the company for inspection prior to the meeting where a written resolution is to be used, these documents must be supplied to all the members either prior to the written resolution or more likely attached to it.

The Articles of Association of most companies allow the directors to pass resolutions in writing (CA 1985, Table A, Reg 93).

7.11 Special Notice

Certain resolutions require special notice to be given to the company, for example:

- the removal of a director (*CA 1985, s 303(2)*, Checklist 6.4);
- appointing a director of a public limited company who has attained the age of 70 (*CA 1985, s 293*);
- Removing an auditor or appointing an auditor other than the retiring auditor (*CA 1985 s 391A(1)*, Checklist 4.18); and
- Filling the casual vacancy in the office of auditor or reappointing a retiring auditor appointed by the directors to fill a casual vacancy (*CA 1985, s 388(3)*, Checklist 4.17).

This is often confused with notice of a special resolution which is something quite different (see Checklist 7.1).

Company Secretary's Handbook reference: CSH 7.40

When preparing a special notice, the following checklist should be considered.

Task:	Reference:	✎
1. Has a signed (usually by an officer) written instrument been served on the company at its registered office and does it:		☐
1.1 detail the nature of the business to which the notice relates; and		☐
1.2 clearly indicate that it is giving the company special notice?		☐
2. Was it received by the company at least 28 days before the meeting at which it is being to be proposed?	*CA 1985, s 379(1)*	☐
3. Has the company given its members notice of such resolution at least 21 days before the meeting?	*CA 1985, s 379(2)*	☐
4. Has notice been given to the individual affected by the resolution, for instance, the director if the special notice related to the proposed removal of a director?		☐

Practical Notes

If, after notice of the intention to move such a resolution has been given to the company, a meeting is called for a date 28 days or less after the notice has been given, the notice is deemed properly given, though not given within the time required (CA 1985, s 379(3)).

Special notice does not give any member a right, which they would not otherwise have, to make the company include a resolution in the agenda for a general meeting. To do so the member must have the right in the Articles of Association or requisition the general meeting (Checklist 7.3).

8 Capital

Contents

8.1   Increase in Share Capital

A company limited by shares or a company limited by guarantee and having a share capital, if authorised by its Articles, may increase the share capital. This gives the opportunity to issue additional shares and raise further funds for the company (see Checklist 8.11).

Company Secretary's Handbook reference: CSH 8.38.

When proposing to increase the share capital of a company, the following checklist should be considered.

Task:	Reference:	✎
1. Have you checked the current authorised share capital of the company?		☐
2. Have you checked the Articles of Association to see if there are any requirements that may affect the increase, for example, are there more than one class of shares and will you need the consent of each class of share for the proposed change?	**Checklist 2.3**	☐
3. Do the directors have the authority to issue the new shares?	*CA 1985, s 80* **Checklist 8.11**	☐
4. Will the existing shareholders have a pre-emption right over the additional authorised shares when issued and, if so, is a waiver of such pre-emption required?	*CA 1985, ss 89, 95* **Checklists 7.1, 7.5, 8.11**	☐
5. Have the board approved the increase in share capital?	**Checklist 6.3**	☐
6. Has the company passed an ordinary resolution to increase the hare capital issued stating:	*CA 1985, s 123(2)* **Checklists 7.1, 7.6, 7.10**	☐
6.1 previous share capital;		☐
6.2 the new share capital;		☐
6.3 the number of new shares and their denomination; and		☐
6.4 the rights of the shares (if different to those already in issue)?	**Checklist 8.17**	☐
7. Have you completed and filed at Companies House the following:	**Checklist 5.1**	☐
7.1 a Form 123;	*CA 1985, s 123(1)*	☐
7.2 an original copy of the ordinary resolution increasing the share capital;	*CA 1985, s 123(3)*	☐
7.3 an amended copy of the Memorandum of Association;	*CA 1985, s 18(2)*	☐
7.4 Articles of Association if amended?	*CA 1985, s 18(2)*	☐

Practical Notes

The capital clause of the Memorandum of Association in a company limited by shares states the number of shares that the company was registered with on incorporation (Checklist 2.1). The share capital may also appear in the Articles of Association (see Checklist 2.3).

When checking the current authorised and issued share capital, it is useful as an initial check to see if it corresponds with the capital note in the last set of accounts.

When an ordinary resolution to increase the capital is passed, it is usual to pass an additional resolution allowing the directors to issue the shares pursuant to section 80 of the Companies Act 1985. In addition, if the intention is to issue the shares to other than existing shareholders (and for private companies if the Articles do not already allow this) then a resolution is passed to disapply the statutory pre-emption rights (see Checklist 8.11 and Checklist 2.3).

When completing Form 123, ensure you either describe the rights of the shares, state that they will rank pari passu with the existing shares or provide that the rights of the shareholders are described in the Articles. It is important that the rights of each class of shares are understood at the outset (see Checklist 8.17).

If you are creating a new class of shares where the Articles of Association are being amended, a special resolution will be required.

Listed companies will need to comply with additional requirements imposed by some institutional investors.

8.2 Bonus Issue

This is also referred to as a scrip issue, or capitalisation of reserves.

This is the mechanism to increase the amount of issued share capital by converting certain reserves into shares. The reason for doing this could be, for instance, to increase the company's issued share capital in order to register as a public company without requiring the shareholders to inject further funds. Unlike a rights issue no additional funds from shareholders are being sought. As such, it is really only an accounting entry that is being made. Issuing redeemable shares that are then redeemed may have some tax advantages in certain circumstances.

Company Secretary's Handbook reference: CSH 8.13.

When proposing that the company has a bonus issue, the following should be considered.

Task:		Reference:	✍
1.	Do the Articles allow the company to capitalise the reserves and do they set down a procedure?	**Checklist 2.3**	☐
2.	Have you calculated the basis of the number of bonus shares to be issued in respect of each share currently held?		☐
3.	Does the company have sufficient authorised share capital of each appropriate class of shares?	**Checklists 8.1, 8.17**	☐
4.	Do the directors have the appropriate authority to issue new shares?	*CA 1985, s 80(1)* **Checklist 8.11**	☐
5.	Do the company's accounts show sufficient reserves available for capitalisation?	*CA 1985, s 263*	☐
6.	Has the board of directors approved the basis of the bonus issue?	**Checklist 6.3**	☐
7.	Have letters of allotment been issued containing:		☐
	7.1 the name of the company;		☐
	7.2 the name of the individual or company receiving the shares; and		☐
	7.3 the number and class of shares?		☐
8.	Has a Form 88(2) been prepared and filed at Companies House?	*CA 1985, s 88(2)* **Checklist 5.1**	☐
9.	Has the register of members been updated to reflect the increase in the number of shares issued?	*CA 1985, s 363* **Checklist 3.1**	☐
10.	Have share certificates been issued?	*CA 1985, s 185(1)* **Checklist 8.15**	☐

Practical Notes

A bonus issue of shares is to the existing shareholders so there is no problem about the pre-emption rights.

The reserves which may be capitalised are, for example, distributable profit or quasi-capital funds such as share premium account or capital redemption reserve.

Most Articles of Association allow companies to capitalise their reserves by way of bonus issue (CA 1985, Table A, Reg 110).

Bonus issues may not be issued at a discount (CA 1985, s 100) and a public company may not allot bonus shares as paid unless they are paid up to at least one quarter of their nominal value (CA 1985, s 101)

Ensure that the capital note in the next set of accounts after the bonus issue reflects the changes that have been made.

Companies House no longer requires a Form 88(3) in respect of a bonus issue. The Form 88(2) needs to make it clear the basis of the allotment of shares.

Listed companies are subject to additional requirements by their regulators.

8.3   Calls on Capital

Shares are sometimes issued without payment being made in full at the time of issue. However, shares cannot be issued at a discount and the price ultimately payable cannot be less than the nominal value of the shares. A call on capital is made when the company wishes to use the unpaid capital.

Apart from the requirement for public companies issuing shares which are a quarter paid up, pursuant to *CA 1985, s 101*, there are no restrictions on issuing partly paid shares. It is usual, for instance, to incorporate companies pursuant to *CA 1985, s 1(2)* without the shares being paid up (see Checklist 2.4).

The checklist set out below should be considered if the company proposes to require the shareholders to pay unpaid monies on their shares. It assumes that the appropriate provisions of *Table A* of the *Companies Act 1985* are in force (these will not have been varied by the majority of private limited companies).

Task: **Reference:**   ✍

1.   Has the board of directors resolved to call up the outstanding   **Checklist 6.3**   ☐
     unpaid share capital?

2.   Has at least 14 clear days notice been given specifying when and   ☐
     where payment is to be made?

3.   Has each shareholder been notified of the details of the call   ☐
     including the amounts that relate to them?

4.   Has the company kept details of payments received and   ☐
     outstanding?

5.   Has each payment been accompanied by the share certificate and   ☐
     has a new share certificate been issued indicating that the shares
     are now fully paid?

6.   Where payment has been received, has the register of members   **Checklist 3.1**   ☐
     been updated to indicate that the shares are now fully paid?

7.   Have the auditors been informed of the call and the monies   ☐
     received?

8.   Have members with outstanding monies due been reminded and   ☐
     warned of the potential interest penalties of non-payment?

Practical Notes

If monies remain outstanding after all notice requirements have been complied with, the Articles of Association should be checked to ascertain the correct procedure, which will probably include forfeiture.

If Table A of the Companies Act 1985 is in place in respect of calls on shares, then the following would apply:

- *If a call remains unpaid after it has become due and payable the directors may give not less than 14 clear days notice requiring payment (including all interest accrued) and stating that the shares will be liable to be forfeited if payment is not received (CA 1985, Table A, Reg 18);*
- *Joint shareholders would be jointly and severally liable to pay the call (CA 1985, Table A, Reg 14);*
- *A call may be required to be made in instalments and may be revoked (in whole or in part) (CA 1985, Table A, Reg 14);*
- *Even if a shareholder transfers his shares he is still liable if the call was made prior to the transfer (CA 1985, Table A, Reg 12); and*

• *Interest may be payable on the outstanding amount unpaid from the day it became due until it is paid at the rate fixed by the terms of allotment of the share or in the notice of the call (CA 1985, Table A, Reg 15).*

8.4   Interim Dividends

This is the usual means of distributing profits by a company to the shareholders. The effect of a dividend is to take money out of the company and return it to the members. Payment can only be made if the company has distributable reserves (*CA 1985, s 263*). The Articles of Association of a company will generally govern the mechanics of paying any dividend. Payments of interim dividends are usually approved by the board of directors between annual general meetings.

Company Secretary's Handbook reference: CSH 7.14

When proposing that an interim dividend be paid, the following issues should be considered.

Task:	**Reference:**	✍
1. Do the Articles of Association allow for the payment of interim dividends?	**Checklist 2.3**	☐
2. Are there appropriate accounts allowing a reasonable judgement on whether the company has distributable reserves and do these accounts include:	*CA 1985, ss 263(3), 270*	☐
2.1 profits, losses, assets and liabilities;		☐
2.2 provisions for, for example, depreciation, diminution in value of assets, retentions to meet liabilities; and		☐
2.3 share capital and reserves (including distributable reserves)?		☐
3. Has the distribution been approved by the company (normally the board of directors)?	**Checklist 6.3**	☐
4. Is this a public company and if so have accounts been prepared and filed at Companies House?	*CA 1985, s 272(2)* **Checklist 5.1**	☐
5. Are dividend warrants and tax vouchers to be prepared unless the dividend is intra-group or if payments are to be made pursuant to bank mandates received straight into the shareholders account?		☐
6. Have you maintained a schedule of payments (including non-cashed cheques)?		☐

Practical Notes

The Articles of Association of most companies allow for the payment of interim dividends (CA 1985, Table A, Reg 103).

In summary private and public companies may make distributions only out of accumulated realised profits (not previously distributed or capitalised less accumulated realised losses not previously written off in a reduction or reorganisation of capital) (CA 1985, s 263(1)–(3)).

As a tax saving measure some firms of accountants are suggesting that companies pay interim dividends more regularly. The directors should be careful not to make an unlawful distribution and should ensure that they have an appropriate accounting system in place.

Many dividend payments, for instance those on preference shares, are made automatically pursuant to the Articles of Association. The Articles of Association need to be reviewed before the payment of dividends (even on ordinary shares) in order to see the procedure to be followed.

There are additional obligations for public limited companies as set out in CA 1985, s 264 on how distributable reserves should be calculated.

A public company may not make a distribution if the company's net assets fall below the aggregate of its called up share capital and undistributable reserves (CA 1985, s 264).

Dividends are paid gross and it is the shareholder's responsibility to account for the income earned.

8.5   Final Dividends

This is the means of distributing profits made by a private limited company to the shareholders based on the year end accounts. Payment can only be made if the company has distributable reserves (*CA 1985, s 263*). The effect of a dividend is to take money out of the company and return it to the members. The process of a company paying a final dividend is usually more onerous than an interim dividend (see Checklist 8.4). The resolution to approve the final dividend is usually tabled for approval at the annual general meeting of the company (see Checklist 7.5).

Company Secretary's Handbook reference: CSH 7.14

When proposing that a final dividend be paid the following should be considered.

Task:		Reference:	✍
1.	Do the Articles of Association allow for the payment of final dividends?	**Checklist 2.3**	☐
2.	Are the latest unqualified audited accounts available?	*CA 1985, s 270*	☐
3.	Are there appropriate accounts allowing a reasonable judgement on whether the company has distributable reserves and do these accounts include:	*CA 1985, ss 263(3), 270*	☐
3.1	profits, losses, assets and liabilities;		☐
3.2	provisions for, for example, depreciation, diminution in value of assets, retentions to meet liabilities;		☐
3.3	share capital and reserves (including distributable reserves)?		☐
4.	Has the distribution been approved by the company in general meeting?	**Checklists 7.2, 7.5**	☐
5.	If the dividend is not intra-group, are dividend warrants (cheques) and tax vouchers to be prepared?		☐
6.	Have you maintained a schedule of payments (including non-cashed cheques)		☐

Practical Notes

In summary, private and public companies may make distributions only out of accumulated realised profits (not previously distributed or capitalised less accumulated realised profits written off in a reduction or reorganisation of capital) (CA 1985, s 263(1)–(3)).

The members at general meeting may reduce the dividend recommended by the directors but not increase it. The directors should be careful to avoid making an unlawful distribution.

If the accounts are qualified by the auditors it will be necessary for the auditors to report to the shareholders that the matter of their qualification is not material for the purpose of declaring the dividend.

If the company has adopted the elective regime, it should consider paying an interim dividend (see Checklist 8.4).

There are additional requirements imposed on public limited companies in respect of how they calculate distributable reserves (CA 1985, s 264).

8.6 Purchase of Own Shares out of Distributable Reserves

Companies may purchase their own shares out of distributable reserves (*CA 1985, s 162*). A purchase of own shares or buyback of shares by a company from its members will reduce the number of shares in issue and the amount of money available to the company. The redemption of shares by a company is dealt with separately (see Checklist 8.8) as is the redemption or purchase of own shares out of capital (see Checklist 8.7).

When proposing to purchase shares out of distributable reserves, the following should be considered.

Task:		Reference:	✍
1.	Do the Articles of Association of the company permit the purchase of its own shares and are there any pre-emption rights that might affect the purchase of own shares?	**Checklist 2.3**	☐
2.	Is it a market or off-market transaction (as there are additional obligations in respect of the off-market purchase of own shares)?	*CA 1985, s 163* **CSH 8.51**	☐
3.	Are the shares fully paid?	*CA 1985, s 159(3)* **Checklist 8.3**	☐
4.	Does the company have sufficient distributable reserves to make the purchase of its own shares?	**Checklist 8.4** **Checklist 8.7**	☐
5.	Has the company passed a special resolution for off-market purchases or an ordinary special resolution for market purchases which:	*CA 1985, ss 164(2), 166(3), 166(6)* **Checklist 7.1** **CSH 8.53, Precedent D, Appendix 8A**	☐
	5.1 specifies the maximum number of shares authorised to be acquired;		☐
	5.2 specifies an authority which is general or limited to the purchase of shares of a particular class or description;		☐
	5.3 determines both the maximum and minimum prices which may be paid for the shares determined by specifying a particular sum or providing a basis or formula for calculating the amount of the price without reference to any person's discretion or opinion; and		☐
	5.4 specifies a date on which it expires, being no later than 18 months after the date of the resolution?		☐
6.	Has the resolution been filed at Companies House within 15 days of its passing?	*CA 1985, s 380(4)(h)* **Checklist 5.1**	☐
7.	Has the company entered into an appropriate contract containing the terms of the purchase and providing for payment on completion?	*CA 1985, ss 164-165*	☐
8.	Is the company a public company? If so, the resolution must specify a date on which the authority is to expire which must not be more than 18 months after the date on which the resolution is passed.	*CA 1985, s 164(4)*	☐

9. Is the resolution, together with a copy of the contract or a memorandum setting out the terms, available to be inspected at the registered office of the company for not less than 15 days ending on the date of the meeting, if the resolution is to be passed at an extraordinary general meeting?   ***CA 1985, s 164(6)***   ☐

10. Has Form 169 been completed and delivered to Companies House within 28 days of the shares being purchased?   **Checklist 5.1**   ☐

11. Has stamp duty been paid on the Form 169?   **Checklist 8.16**   ☐

12. Have copies been kept of any contracts for off market purchases which have completed within the last ten years?   ***CA 1985, s 169(4)***   ☐

Practical Notes

The Articles of Association of most private limited companies will allow for the purchase of own shares subject to the provisions of the Companies Act 1985 (CA 1985, Table A, Reg 35).

The shares that are the subject of the purchase are disenfranchised for the vote on the special resolution. A vendor shareholder who holds shares other than those to be purchased can only vote on a poll in respect of the shares which are not subject to buyback arrangements (CA 1985, s 164(5)).

If the company is a single member company the written resolution procedure will not be available and a general meeting will need to be held to approve the buyback and the agreement (CA 1985, s 164(5) and CA 1985, Sch 15A, para 5(2)). An alternative is to transfer one share to a third party, pass the written resolution and transfer the share back to the majority shareholder.

At the time of passing of the special resolution of the company the agreement for the purchase of the shares needs to be present whether the resolution is to be passed by a general meeting or written resolution (CA 1985, Sch 15A, para 5(3)). If the resolution is to be passed by the company in general meeting the agreement needs to be kept at the registered office for at least 15 clear days prior to the general meeting (CA 1985, s 164(6)).

Only fully paid shares may be bought back (CA 1985, s 159(3)). The buyback cannot go ahead if only redeemable shares would be left (CA 1985, s 162(3)).

The Listing Rules of the UK Listing Authority have specific detailed provisions relating to the purchase by a company of its own shares (see Checklist 7.5). In addition, the Association of British Insurers have issued guidance for listed companies on this matter and may need to be consulted depending on the individual circumstances surrounding a company purchasing its own shares.

8.7   Purchase of Own Shares out of Capital

This procedure is similar to the market purchase by a company of its own shares out of distributable reserves and is a means by which money advanced to the company by the shareholders may be returned (see Checklist 8.6). When there are no reserves that are attributable to shareholders then this procedure may be an option.

However, it is complicated and should only be undertaken by those having sufficient expertise or who have access to legal advice in this area.

When proposing to make a purchase of own shares out of capital, the following should be considered.

Task:	Reference:	✍
1. Is the company a private company (as a public company cannot make a purchase of own shares out of capital)?	*CA 1985, s 171(1)*	☐
2. Does the company have the power under its Articles of Association to purchase its own shares (which does not conflict with any pre-emption restrictions)?	**Checklist 2.3**	☐
3. Has the permissible capital payment been calculated using accounts not more than three months old?	*CA 1985, s 171(3)*	☐
4. Have the directors made a statutory declaration, in the form of Form 173, specifying the amount of the permissible capital repayment and in doing so have they formed the opinion that:	*CA 1985, s 173(3)*	☐
4.1 there will be no grounds on which the company could be found unable to pay its debts immediately following the payment out of capital; and		☐
4.2 as regards to the company's prospects for the year immediately following payment, that it will continue to carry on business as a going concern and be able to pay its debts as they fall due?		☐
5. Did the statutory declaration have annexed to it a report addressed to all the directors by the company's auditor stating that:	*CA 1985, s 173(5)*	☐
5.1 they have inquired into the company's state of affairs;		☐
5.2 the amount specified in the declaration as the permissible capital payment has been properly calculated; and		☐
5.3 they are not aware of anything to indicate that the directors' view as set out in the statutory declaration is unreasonable?		☐
6. Has the payment out of capital been approved by a special resolution of the company, passed within a week of the date on which the directors made the statutory declaration?	*CA 1985, ss 164(2), 174(1)* **Checklist 7.1** **CSH 8.63**	☐
7. Has the resolution been filed at Companies House within 15 days of its passing?	*CA 1985, s 380(1)*	☐

8. Has the company entered into an appropriate contract containing the terms of the purchase and providing for payment on completion? *CA 1985, s 164(6)* ☐

9. Is the statutory declaration and auditors' report available for inspection at the meeting at which the resolution is passed or, if it is proposed that a written resolution procedure will be used, has each member at or before the time when the resolution is to be executed by them, been provided with copies of the same? *CA 1985, s 174(4)* ☐

10. Is the resolution, together with a copy of the contract or a memorandum setting out the terms, available to be inspected at the registered office of the company for not less than 15 days ending on the date of the meeting, if the resolution is to be passed at an extraordinary general meeting? *CA 1985, s 164(6)* ☐

11. Has there been a notice published in the London Gazette within one week of the passing of the special resolution for payment out of capital: *CA 1985, s 175(1)* ☐

    11.1 stating that the company has approved a payment out of capital for the purpose of acquiring its own shares; ☐

    11.2 specifying the amount of the permissible capital payment for the shares and the date of the resolution; ☐

    11.3 stating that the statutory declaration of the directors' and the auditors' reports are available for inspection at the company's registered office; and ☐

    11.4 stating that any creditor of the company may, at any time within the five weeks immediately following the date of the special resolution, apply to the court for an order prohibiting the payment? ☐

12. Has a similar announcement been placed in an appropriate national newspaper, or notice been given to each of the creditors of the company within the same one week period following the passing of the special resolution for payment out of capital? *CA 1985, ss 175(2), (3)* ☐

13. Has a copy of the statutory declaration (Form 173) and the auditors' report been filed at Companies House by the time of the earlier notice in the London Gazette, the advertisement in the national newspaper, or the notice to all of the creditors? *CA 1985, s 175(4) and (5)* **Checklist 5.1** ☐

14. Has Form 169 been completed and delivered to Companies House within 28 days of the shares being purchased? **Checklist 5.1** ☐

15. Has stamp duty been paid on the Form 169? **Checklist 8.16** ☐

16. Have copies been kept of any contracts for off market purchases which have completed within the last ten years? *CA 1985, s 169(4)* ☐

17. Has the register of members been updated to reflect the redemption? **Checklist 3.1** ☐

Practical Notes

The Articles of Association of most companies will allow for the purchase of own shares subject to the provision of the Companies Act 1985 (CA 1985, Table A, Reg 35). It is preferable that they should not prevent financial assistance being given.

The permissible capital payment is the amount of the total repayment less any available profits of the company and the proceeds of any fresh issue of shares made for the purpose of the redemption or purchase.

There are special rules contained in section 172 of the Companies Act 1985 for determining the availability of profits. Practically, most companies will attempt this procedure soon after the year end when their audited accounts are available for the directors to base their judgement about the company and its reserves.

The members holding the shares to which the resolution relates are disenfranchised from voting on the special resolution pursuant to section 174(2) and (3) of the Companies Act 1985.

If the company is a single member company the written resolution procedure will not be available and a general meeting will need to be held to approve the buyback and the agreement (CA 1985, s 164(5) and CA 1985, Sch 15A, para 5(2)). An alternative is to transfer one share to a third party, pass the written resolution and transfer the share back to the majority shareholder.

At the time of passing of the special resolution of the company the agreement for the purchase of the shares needs to be present whether the resolution is to be passed by a general meeting or written resolution (CA 1985, Sch 15A, para 5(3)). If the resolution is to be passed by the company in general meeting the agreement needs to be kept at the registered office for at least 15 clear days prior to the general meeting (CA 1985, s 164(6)).

Only fully paid shares may be bought back (CA 1985, s 159(3)). The buyback cannot go ahead if only redeemable shares would be left (CA 1985, s 162(3)).

The purchase of own shares will be reflected in the next accounts for the company in the creation of a capital redemption reserve.

8.8   Redemption of Shares

It is not unusual for a company to issue redeemable shares and *sections 159* and *160* of the *Companies Act 1985* contain the provisions by which a company can issue and redeem such shares. Redeeming shares is a mechanism of returning capital to the shareholders.

See also Checklist 8.6 and Checklist 8.7.

When proposing to redeem shares, the following should be considered.

Task:	Reference:	✍
1. Were the shares to be redeemed originally issued as redeemable shares?	*CA 1985, s 159(1)*	☐
2. Did the company have the power under its Articles of Association to issue redeemable shares?	*CA 1985, s 159(1)* **Checklist 2.3**	☐
3. Have you ensured that when the shares were issued, there were some non-redeemable shares in issue?	*CA 1985, s 159(2)* **Checklist 8.1**	☐
4. Are the shares fully paid?	*CA 1985, s 159(3)* **Checklist 8.3**	☐
5. Are the shares to be redeemed out of distributable profits or a fresh issue of shares made for the purpose of the redemption?	*CA 1985, s 160(1)(a)* **Checklist 8.4**	☐
6. Has the redemption been approved by the board of directors or by such other mechanism as required by the Articles of Association?	**Checklists 2.3, 6.3**	☐
7. Has a Form 122 been completed and filed at Companies House?	**Checklist 5.1**	☐
8. Have the share certificates been received and cancelled?	**Checklist 8.15**	☐
9. Have the monies been paid to the shareholders?		☐
10. Has the register of members been updated to reflect the redemption?	**Checklist 3.1**	☐

Practical Notes

Most Articles of Association will give the company power to issue redeemed shares (CA 1985, Table A, Reg3).

Section 159A of the Companies Act 1985 (inserted by section 133(2) of the Companies Act 1989), sets out conditions as regards the terms and manner of redemption which must be satisfied before redeemable shares may be issued. However these have not yet been brought into force.

For shares to be redeemed they have to have been originally issued as redeemable shares. Similarly no redeemable shares may be issued at a time when there are no issued shares of the company which are non-redeemable (CA 1985, s 159(2)).

Any redemption of shares will be reflected in the next accounts for the company in the creation of a capital redemption reserve.

Companies may redeem shares out of capital rather than distributable reserves but the company will be subject to similar procedures as a purchase of own shares out of capital (CA 1985, s 171).

8.9　Financial Assistance

There is a general prohibition on companies giving financial assistance directly or indirectly for the acquisition or the proposed acquisition of its own shares, if the financial assistance is for the purpose of that acquisition (and any liability has been incurred in connection with such acquisition) (*CA 1985, s 151*). Companies are also prohibited from giving financial assistance after the acquisition of shares, where the assistance is directly or indirectly for the purpose of reducing or discharging a liability incurred for the acquisition.

The restriction in *section 151* of the *Companies Act 1985* only applies to companies incorporated in Great Britain. Checklists 8.6-8.8 are all exceptions to these restrictions and are dealt with separately.

Currently this is one of the more complex areas of the *Companies Act 1985*. However, it appears likely it will be simplified pursuant to the Final Report of the Company Law Review.

When considering if something is financial assistance, firstly determine whether there is an acquisition of shares. An acquisition of shares includes the issue of new shares, not just the transfer of existing shares. *Section 152(1)* of the *Companies Act 1985* goes on to define prohibited financial assistance.

In addition, the following should be considered in respect of financial assistance.

Task:		Reference:	✍
1.	Is the company doing something that falls into one of these categories set out in the *Companies Act 1985*:		☐
1.1	financial assistance given by way of a gift;	*CA 1985, s 152(1)(a)(i)*	☐
1.2	financial assistance given by way of guarantee, security or indemnity, other than an indemnity in respect of the indemnifier's own neglect or default, or by way of release or waiver;	*CA 1985, s 152(1)(a)(ii)*	☐
1.3	financial assistance given by way of loan or other agreement under which any of the obligations of the person giving the assistance are to be fulfilled at a time when in accordance with the agreement any obligation of another party to the agreement remains unfulfilled, or by way of the novation of, the assignment of the rights arising under the loan or such other agreement; or	*CA 1985, s 152(1)(a)(iii)*	☐
1.4	any other financial assistance given by a company the net assets of which are thereby reduced to a material extent or which has no net assets?	*CA 1985, s 152(1)(a)(iv)* **CSH 8.66**	☐
2.	Does the financial assistance fall into one of the exemptions set out in *CA 1985, s 153(3)*:		☐
2.1	Is it a distribution of a company's assets by way of dividend lawfully made or a distribution made in the course of the company's winding-up;	*CA 1985, s 153(3)(a)* **Checklists 8.4, 8.5**	☐
2.2	the allotment of bonus shares;	*CA 1985, s 153(3)(b)*	☐
2.3	a reduction of capital confirmed by order of the court under *CA 1985, s 137*;	*CA 1985, s 153(3)(c)*	☐

2.4 a reduction or purchase of the company's own shares; — *CA 1985, s 153(3)(d)* **Checklists 8.6, 8.7** ☐

2.5 anything done in pursuance of an order of the court under *CA 1985, s 425* (compromises and arrangements with creditors and members); — *CA 1985, s 153(3)(e)* ☐

2.6 anything done under an arrangement made in pursuance of *section 110* of the *Insolvency Act 1986* (acceptance of shares by liquidator in winding up as consideration for sale of property), or anything done under an arrangement made between a company and its creditors which is binding on the creditors by virtue of *Part 1* of the *Insolvency Act 1986*; — *CA 1985, ss 153(3)(f), 154(3)(g)* **CSH 8.67** ☐

2.7 is it for the purpose of an employee share scheme in good faith for the benefit of the company; — *CA 1985, s 153 (4)(b)* **CSH 8.68** ☐

2.8 a loan by the company to an employee (other than a director) employed in good faith by the company to enable them to acquire fully paid shares in the company, or its holding company to be held by them by way of beneficial ownership? — *CA 1985, s 153(4)(c)* **CSH 8.69** ☐

Whitewash Procedure:

3. Is it a private company? If so then following the 'Whitewash' procedure under *sections 155–158* of the *Companies Act 1985* may be possible. ☐

4. Does the company have net assets which will not be reduced or, to the extent that they are reduced, will the assistance be provided out of distributable profits? ☐

5. Have each of the directors satisfied themselves that they are of the view that: — *CA 1985, s 156(2)* **CSH 8.73** ☐

   5.1 the relevant group company's assets exceed its liabilities (including its contingent and prospective liabilities); ☐

   5.2 there will be no grounds on which the relevant group company could be found to be unable to pay its debts immediately following the giving of the assistance in question and will be able to pay its debts as they fall due in the following year; ☐

   5.3 or, if it is intended to wind up the company within twelve months of the date of the statutory declaration, that the relevant group company will be able to pay its debts in full within twelve months of the winding up? ☐

6. Have the directors sworn a statutory declaration in front of a solicitor or commissioner for oaths on Form 155(6)(a) or (b), giving details of the assistance to be given? — *CA 1985, s 155(6)* **CSH 8.73** ☐

7. Do you have a report addressed to the directors from the auditors stating that they have enquired into the state of affairs of the company and that they are not aware of anything to indicate that the — *CA 1985, s 156(4)* ☐

directors' opinion in the statutory declaration is unreasonable in all the circumstances?

8. Is the company a wholly owned subsidiary? If not, then the financial assistance must be approved by special resolution in general meeting.

    Checklist 7.1 ☐

9. Have the shareholders approved the financial assistance by special resolution within seven days of the financial assistance?

    CA 1985, s 157(1) ☐
    Checklists 7.1, 7.2, 7.10
    CSH 8.72

10. Has a copy of the statutory declaration and auditors' report been made available for inspection at the extraordinary general meeting or, if the resolution was passed by written resolution, circulated to each member?

    ☐

11. Have all the members approved the resolution, in which case the financial assistance may be given immediately, otherwise you will have to wait four weeks from the passing of the resolution (but may not be given more than eight weeks after)?

    CA 1985, s 158(2) ☐

12. Have the form(s) 155(6)(a) or (b), the auditors' report and the special resolution been filed at Companies House within 15 days of the making of the statutory declaration?

    CA 1985, s 156(5) ☐
    Checklist 5.1

Practical Notes

Section 154 of the Companies Act 1985 states that there are special restrictions for public companies. They may only give financial assistance if the company has net assets which are not thereby reduced or, to the extent that those assets are thereby reduced if the assistance is provided out of distributable profits (CSH 8.70).

Exempt employee share schemes would include, for example, schemes for bone fide employees or former employees of that company or of another company in the same group or the wives, husbands, widows, widowers, children or stepchildren under the age of 18 of any such employee or former employee.

If the financial assistance to be given by the company is or was for the purpose of the acquisition or proposed acquisition of shares in the holding company of the company, then the directors of both the holding company and the company itself would need to complete statutory declarations on either Form 155(6)(a) or (b).

There is also a maximum time in which the financial assistance must be given which is eight weeks from the date on which the directors of the company made their statutory declaration or, if more than one declaration was given by a group of companies, the date on which the earliest of the statutory declarations was made (CA 1985, s 158(4)) unless the court, on a application under CA 1985, s 157, orders otherwise.

8.10   Power of Attorney

Powers of attorney are an invaluable tool in allowing authority to be delegated. It enables another person or persons to act on your or your company's behalf. The power granted pursuant to a power of attorney can be restricted to certain specific purposes or contain a more general power.

There are two types of powers of attorney, the general power of attorney governed by the *Powers of Attorney Act 1971* and the enduring power of attorney governed by the *Enduring Powers of Attorney Act 1985*. This second type is only applicable to individuals and is not to be considered here.

When a company is considering appointing a power of attorney, the following are questions that could be asked.

Task:	Reference:	✍
1. Has the power of attorney been executed as a deed?	***Powers of Attorney Act 1971, s 1(1)*** **Checklist 3.8**	☐
2. Do the Articles of Association allow the company to appoint agents?	**Checklist 2.3**	☐
3. If a company is being appointed as the attorney, does the Memorandum of Association allow such company to act as an attorney?	**Checklist 2.2**	☐
4. Does the power of attorney contain:		☐
4.1 the identity of the attorney or attorneys (if more than one attorney is appointed, the power may be joint, or joint and several, and must be stated clearly);		☐
4.2 an accurate description of the nature and extent of the attorney's authority – an agreement between the attorney and a third party will only bind the donor of the power if it was within the attorney's authority to enter into such an agreement;		☐
4.3 the duration of the power of attorney; and		☐
4.4 any provisions relating to ratification?		☐

Practical Notes

The Articles of Association will allow a company to appoint an agent (CA 1985, Table A, Reg 71).

There is no definition of who may be a donor (the person giving the power) and, consequently, common law and general contractual provisions apply. Both individuals and companies may appoint an attorney to act on their behalf.

Companies, as well as individuals, can also be attorneys. A corporate attorney will nominate one of its officers to fulfil the duties of the attorney.

Powers of attorney are used, for instance, to enable buyers of shares to obtain certain rights prior to registration when the legal title in the shares acquired will be transferred to them. Under an incomplete share purchase agreement the seller holds the shares as a fiduciary of the buyer. However, the seller is not obliged to vote those shares in accordance with the buyer's wishes. Under a power of attorney, the buyer can sign written resolutions, receive notices of meetings, accept short notice, appoint a proxy, attend meetings and, significantly, exercise voting rights as if he were the registered shareholder.

Directors can use powers of attorney, for example, to:

- *execute documents in the absence of a company representative. It provides confirmation that the signatory has authority to act on behalf of the company;*
- *execute a deed in the United Kingdom or abroad. Usually two corporate officers are required to execute a deed on behalf of a company, however, an individual attorney may be appointed to act on the company's behalf (CA 1985, s 38 (1) and (2)); or*
- *appoint proxies.*

It is advisable to revoke a power of attorney by deed (see Checklist 3.8).

Extension of powers can not be agreed informally. It will be necessary to execute another power of attorney to grant new or increased powers.

The donor will normally indemnify the attorney fully against all costs, liabilities etc. which the attorney incurs whilst fulfilling his duties.

8.11   Applications and Allotments

This is the mechanism for bringing new shares into issue. Often this will directly follow on from an increase in share capital (see Checklist 8.1). If new shares are issued, it will increase the amount of capital available for use by the company.

Care needs to be taken as the directors may not allot additional shares unless they have specific authority.

Bonus issues and rights issues are specific types of allotments of shares (see Checklist 8.2).

Company Secretary's Handbook reference: CSH 8.4.

When proposing to issue additional shares, the following should be considered.

Task:	Reference:	✍
1. Does the company have sufficient authorised but unissued shares available for the allotment?	**Checklist 8.1**	☐
2. Who has the requisite authority to issue shares pursuant to the Articles of Association?	**Checklist 2.3**	☐
3. Do the directors have the power to issue shares? Unless the company has made an election pursuant to *CA 1985, s 80A* to have an enduring authority, this authority must be given by resolution of the company or, alternatively in the case of a private company, contained in the Articles of Association. This power must contain:	**Checklists 2.3, 7.5, 7.7**	☐
3.1 the maximum amount of the shares that may be allotted (which must be a date no later than five years after the authority is granted); and	*CA 1985, s 80(4)*	☐
3.2 the expiry date of the authority.	*CA 1985, s 80(4)*	☐
4. Who are the shares to be offered to and, if they are to be issued to persons other than the existing shareholders (pro rata), is there an effective disapplication of pre-emption rights in place?	*CA 1985, ss 89–95* **Checklists 2.3, 7.5, 8.1** **CSH 8.5**	☐
5. Has the board (or members if pre-emption rights are in place) approved a letter of application containing:	**Checklist 6.3**	☐
5.1 the name of the company;		☐
5.2 the name of the individual or company to whom the offer is being made;		☐
5.3 the number of shares and class of shares being offered;		☐
5.4 the amount payable and the timescale for receipt; and		☐
5.5 clarity that completion of the letter of allotment and satisfactory payment will be treated as an application for shares?		☐

6. Has the letter of application been circulated to the relevant parties? ☐

7. Has a completed letter of application been received in respect of all of the proposed new shares? ☐

8. Have the monies (or non-cash consideration been received)? **CSH 8.8** ☐

9. Has the board of directors resolved to issue the shares and appropriate share certificate to the applicants? **Checklist 6.3** ☐

10. Have appropriate entries been made in the register of members and register of allotments? **CA 1985, s 352** **Checklist 3.1** ☐

11. Has an appropriate share certificate been issued to each successful applicant? **CA 1985, s 185(1)** **Checklist 8.15** ☐

12. Has a Form 88(2) been filed at Companies House within 28 days of the allotment of the shares? **CA 1985, s 88(2)(a)** **Checklist 5.1** ☐

13. If this an allotment for a non-cash consideration has either a Form 88(3) or a copy of the agreement constituting the title of the allottee to the allotment been filed at Companies House? **CA 1985, s 88(2)(b)** **Checklist 5.1** ☐

Practical Notes

The most common error on issuing shares is failing to have an appropriate authority in place to issue the shares (see Checklist 8.1). Do not rely solely on your auditors to make this judgement!

When shares are issued for a non-cash consideration Companies House will expect to see either Form 88(3) or an agreement which, in many circumstances, will need to be stamped or adjudicated as non stampable (see Checklist 8.16).

There are additional restrictions on public companies issuing shares for non-cash considerations (CSH 8.10).

When checking the disapplication of pre-emption rights note that a plc must disapply these by special resolution whereas a private company can disapply CA 1985, s 89(1) by provision in its Articles of Association.

Private companies limited by shares may not make offers to the public for shares. Both the company and the directors would lay themselves open to the possibility of a fine pursuant to CA 1985, s 81(2) for so doing. The public in this context is hard to define, one view is that an offer to apply for shares made to more than fifty people would constitute an offer being made to the public.

Shares can be issued without payment being made in full at the time of issue. However, shares cannot be issued at a discount and the price ultimately payable cannot be less than the nominal value. A call on capital is made when the company wishes to use any unpaid capital (see Checklist 8.3).

8.12　Consolidation, Sub-division and Cancellation

A company may alter its share capital in accordance with *Companies Act 1985, section 121*. This may be by, for instance, sub-dividing each share of £1 into ten shares of 10p or a similar consolidation. Changes of this type can be for a variety of reasons and it is difficult to generalise.

The following are questions to consider when undertaking a consolidation, sub-division or cancellation of shares.

Task:	Reference:	✍
1.　Do the Articles of Association allow the company to make the proposed change?	**Checklist 2.3**	☐
2.　Will the proposed change vary the class rights of the shares and hence need class consents?	**Checklist 8.17**	☐
3.　Has the company passed the appropriate resolution?	**Checklists 7.1, 7.6** **CSH 8.39–8.42**	☐
4.　Has a Form 122 been sent to Companies House within one month?	*CA 1985, s 122* **Checklist 5.1** **CSH 8.43**	☐
5.　Has the register of members been updated to reflect the change?	**Checklist 3.1**	☐
6.　Have new share certificates been issued (if required)?	**Checklist 8.15**	☐

Practical Notes

Cancellation of shares usually relates to unissued shares and should not be confused with a purchase of own shares.

Redenomination of shares where the nominal value of the shares has not varied would not require a Form 122 to be filed, however, the resolution making the change in share rights should be filed at Companies House.

8.13 Transfer of Shares

This is one of the most common procedures a company secretary must undertake and should usually be straightforward. It is fundamental that it is dealt with correctly to ensure that the owners of the company are clearly known.

The transfer involves the passing of shares owned by one member of the company to either a new or pre-existing member.

When proposing to register a transfer of shares, the following should be considered.

Task:	Reference:	✍
1. Do you have an appropriate form of transfer (the form most commonly used is set out in the *Stock Transfer Act 1963* i.e. the stock transfer form):	*CA 1985, s 183(1)* **CSH 7.16; Appendix 7B**	☐
1.1 is the person transferring the shares entered in the register of members as the holder of the shares;	**CSH 7.17**	☐
1.2 is the stock transfer form either stamped or certified on the reverse as non-stampable;	**Checklist 8.16** **CSH 7.19**	☐
1.3 is the class of shares given on the stock transfer form the same as in the register of members;		☐
1.4 is the number of shares the same on the stock transfer form as in the register of members; and		☐
1.5 is the stock transfer form properly executed?	**Checklist 3.8** **CSH Appendix 7B, Precedent A2**	☐
2. Is the share certificate in respect of the holding being submitted to the company or an appropriate letter of indemnity?	*CA 1985, s 185* **Checklist 8.15**	☐
3. Are there any impediments to the transfer which are noted in the register of members (e.g. court orders)?	**CSH 7.17**	☐
4. Are there any particular restrictions on transferring the shares in the Articles of Association, for instance, do they need to be offered to the existing shareholders?	**Checklist 2.3** **CSH 7.18**	☐
5. Has the transfer been approved by the board or a properly appointed committee of the board?	**Checklist 6.3**	☐
6. Has the register of members been updated (most companies also maintain a register of transfers though this is not a statutory requirement) and is the date of entry to the register of members the latest of the date the:	*CA 1985, s 352* **Checklist 3.1**	☐
6.1 stock transfer form is executed;	**Checklist 3.8**	☐
6.2 stock transfer form is approved by the board of directors; and	**Checklist 6.3**	☐

6.3   stamp duty is paid?   **Checklist 8.16**   ☐

7.   Have you issued a new share certificate within two months of   *CA 1985, s 185*   ☐
      registration of the transfer?   **Checklist 8.15**
                                                                          CSH 7.24

Practical Notes

It is an offence to register the transfer of a share without a properly completed transfer document being presented to the company (CA 1985, s 183(1)).

There are restrictions on the nature of the transfer document in part to ensure that stamp duty is paid (CSH Appendix 7A and Checklist 8.16).

The most common mistake with the register of members is for the transfer to be entered in the register prior to the document being stamped. The proper date of entry should be the latest date it was approved by the board of directors, the date the stock transfer form was completed or the date it was stamped. Theoretically any of these could be the latest (see Checklist 3.1).

The other common mistake on the transfer of shares is to leave the subscribers shares or not to properly transfer them to the correct recipient. Once such shares have been brought into issue in this way they should entirely be treated like any other, and will need to be paid up at some stage (see Checklist 8.3).

Companies are not normally required to execute stock transfer forms as a deed or under seal though if there is no consideration they should (Checklist 3.8).

For unpaid shares both the transferee and transferor should execute the transfer as the transferee is taking on a liability.

There is no requirement to number paid up shares, so if the shares have been paid up then the board should resolve that the shares shall not be numbered.

Listed companies, subject to the UK Listing Authority's Listing Rules, will probably have dematerialised their share certificates by entering CREST, so that there is no longer the requirement to, for instance, issue a share certificate. Transfers by such companies will normally be dealt with by registrars and the procedure for the transfer of shares and the payment of duty thereon is different.

If the company refuses to register a transfer of shares it must notify the transferee within two months of the company receiving the transfer (CA 1985, s 183(5)).

There are often restrictions in the Articles of Association in respect of the transfer of shares, particularly in respect of companies which are joint ventures. These need to be read carefully and complied with.

8.14   Transmission of Shares

Transmission is what happens when shares are transferred by operation of law. It is similar in nature to a transfer of shares (see Checklist 8.13). The most common reason would be the death of the shareholder though it could occur, for instance, on bankruptcy or because the individual has become of unsound mind under the *Mental Health Act 1983* and become subject of an order of the Court of Protection. On the death of a shareholder the legal title to the shares passes to the personal representatives or, if the shares are jointly held, to the surviving holder. Due to the differing causes of the transmission, it is only really possible to give a general checklist.

When documentation is received by the company in relation to such a matter, the following should be checked.

Task:	Reference:	✎
1. Have the Articles been checked to see if they specify what should happen to the shares in the particular circumstances?	**Checklist 2.3**	☐
2. Has the company received a letter of request from the personal representatives, the trustee in bankruptcy or the receiver to register them as the owner of the shares, or has the receiver registered his appointment and have any relevant orders been registered with the company secretary?		☐
3. Has sufficient documentation been produced for the transmission to take place (i.e. grant of probate, letter of administration, stock transfer form)?		☐
4. Are the details of the shareholder concerned the same on both the documents submitted, the register of members and the share certificate?		☐
5. Is the company secretary satisfied that the documents are genuine?		☐
6. Has the receipt of the documents been entered into the register of members (if appropriate) and the document endorsed?	*CA 1983, s 352* **Checklist 3.1**	☐
7. Has the share certificate been endorsed in favour of the new shareholder or a new certificate been issued?	**Checklist 8.15**	☐
8. Have the documents and appropriate share certificate been returned to the shareholder?		☐

Practical Notes

CSH 7.23 A-P set out the circumstances that documentation may be presented on the company and the actions to be taken in respect of, for instance, letters of administration, letters of request, and court orders.

8.15 Share Certificates

Share certificates are prima facie proof of ownership of shares in a company (*CA 1985, s 186*).

Share certificates need to clearly identify the shares and the holder of them. If shares are to be issued please refer to Checklist 8.11 or, if shares have been transferred, please refer to Checklist 8.13.

When issuing a share certificate the following issues should be considered.

Task:	Reference:	✍
1. Does the share certificate include:	**CSH 7.24**	☐
1.1 the full name of the shareholder (for joint shareholders only the first named is usually required, however, it is best practice to show them all);		☐
1.2 a sequential serial number;		☐
1.3 the name (and number) of the company;		☐
1.4 the name of the registered holder;		☐
1.5 the number and description of shares;		☐
1.6 a statement to the extent to which the shares are paid up;		☐
1.7 the date of issue. and		☐
1.8 in the case of joint holders, the address of the first named person may be included.		☐
2. Do the entries on the share certificate correspond with the entries in the register of members?	**Checklist 3.1**	☐
3. In respect of the share details which appear on the share certificate, are you sure that:		☐
3.1 there has never been a share certificate in respect of these shares; or		☐
3.2 all previous share certificates in respect of the shares have been cancelled; or		☐
3.3 the company has received appropriate indemnities in respect of all relevant lost share certificates?		☐
4. Has the issuing of the share certificate been approved by the board of directors who may have delegated their authority?	**Checklist 6.3**	☐

5. Has the share certificate been properly executed by the company   *CA 1985, s 186*   ☐
    in accordance with the Articles of Association (usually under seal   **Checklist 3.8**
    or executed on behalf of the company)?   **CSH 7.24**

6. Has the share certificate been issued by the company within two   *CA 1985, s 185(1)*   ☐
    months of the allotment or transfer of shares?   **Checklist 8.11**
    Checklist 8.14

Practical Notes

Most listed companies, subject to the UK Listing Authority's Listing Rules, have joined the CREST system and for these companies there is no obligation to issue a certificate in respect of uncertified shares. CREST is the electronic settlement system that allows shareholders to transfer their securities in dematerialised form.

In the case of lost share certificates the member should be requested to search for the certificate and confirm whether or not it has been found. If the certificate cannot be found the member should be asked to provide the company with an indemnity (in order to protect the company). On receipt of the indemnity, the company should allocate a duplicate certificate (with a different issued number to avoid confusion) and record what has happened in the statutory records.

If a share certificate has been lost then the company should forward to the shareholder an appropriate indemnity as mentioned above. This is principally to protect the company in case of fraud. In the case of listed companies, they may need to be guaranteed by a bank or insurance company. This is an area where the company can show some discretion as to what is required to safeguard their interests.

8.16   Stamp Duty

The issue of stamp duty arises on any transfer of shares including a purchase of own shares. A transfer may attract stamp duty payable on the total consideration; a fixed rate of stamp duty; or total exemption from stamp duty. It is an offence for a company to enter in the register of members a transfer unless it is received on a proper instrument of transfer, for example, a stock transfer form (*CA 1985, s 183(1)*). Similarly, share certificates may only be issued following a transfer of shares which is duly stamped or adjudicated as exempt from stamp duty (*CA 1985, s 185(1)*).

When presented with a stock transfer for stamping, the following should be considered.

Task:	Reference:	✍
1. Does the transfer fall into any of the following categories which are exempt from stamp duty, for instance:	**Stamp Duty (Exempt Instruments) Regulations 1987 (SI 1987/516)**	☐
1.1 is it a vesting of property subject to a trust in the trustees of the trust on the appointment of a new trustee, or in the continuing trustees on the retirement of a trustee;		☐
1.2 is it a conveyance or transfer of property the subject of a specific devise or legacy to the beneficiary named in the will (or his nominee);		☐
1.3 is it a conveyance or transfer of property which forms part of an intestate's estate to the person entitled on intestacy (or his nominee);		☐
1.4 is it the appropriation of property which *section 84(4)* of the *Finance Act 1985* (death: appropriation in satisfaction of a general legacy of money) or *FA 1985, s 84(5)* or *(7)* (death: appropriation in satisfaction of any interest of surviving spouse and in Scotland also of any interest of issue);		☐
1.5 is it a conveyance or transfer of property which forms part of the residuary estate of a testator to a beneficiary (or his nominee) entitled solely by virtue of his entitlement under the will;		☐
1.6 is it a conveyance or transfer of property out of settlement in or towards satisfaction of a beneficiary's interest, not being an interest acquired for money or money's worth, being a conveyance or transfer constituting a distribution of property in accordance with the provisions of the settlement;		☐
1.7 is it a conveyance or transfer of property on and in consideration only of marriage to a party to the marriage (or his nominee) or to trustees to be held on the terms of a settlement made in consideration only of the marriage;		☐
1.8 is it a conveyance or transfer of property within *FA 1985, s 83(1)* (transfer in connection with divorce etc.);		☐

1.9   is it a conveyance or transfer by the liquidator of property which formed part of the assets of the company in liquidation to a shareholder of that company (or his nominee) in or towards satisfaction of the shareholder's rights on a winding-up; ☐

1.10   is it a grant in fee simple of an easement in or over land for no consideration in money or money's worth; ☐

1.11   is it a conveyance or transfer of property operating as a voluntary disposition *inter vivos* for no consideration in money or money's worth nor any consideration referred to in *section 57* of the *Stamp Act 1891* (conveyance in consideration of a debt etc.); or ☐

1.12   is it a conveyance or transfer of property by an instrument within *FA 1985, s 84(1)* (death: varying disposition)? ☐

2.   If the transfer does fall into one of the exempt categories set out in question 1, has the relevant certificate been completed and signed on the reverse of the stock transfer form? ☐

3.   If the transfer is not exempt, does it fall into any of the following categories giving rise to a fixed rate of stamp duty of £5: ☐

3.1   are the shares being transferred as security for a loan or as a re-transfer back to the original transferor on repayment of a loan; or ☐

3.2   are the shares being transferred: ☐

     3.2.1   to a nominee of the transferor; ☐

     3.2.2   a nominee back to the original transferor as the beneficial owner; or ☐

     3.2.3   one nominee to another nominee of the same beneficial owner where the shares have always been held on behalf of that beneficial owner? ☐

4.   If the transfer does fall into one of the fixed rate categories set out in question 3, has the relevant certificate been completed and signed on the reverse of the stock transfer form? ☐

5.   If the transfer does not fall into any of the aforementioned categories, is it possible to gain exemption from stamp duty either because it is broadly a transfer where: *Finance Act (FA) 1930, s 42* ☐

5.1   a transferor directly or indirectly beneficially owns 75% of the ordinary share capital of the transferee, or vice versa? or ☐

5.2   a third company (the 'common parent') directly or indirectly beneficially owns 75% of the ordinary share capital of both. ☐

6.   If the transfer does not fall into any of the aforementioned   *FA 1986, s 75*   ☐
categories, is it possible to gain exemption from stamp duty
because it is broadly a transfer where:

    6.1   a company (the 'acquiring company'), often a new   ☐
company, is acquiring the whole or part of the
undertaking of an existing company (the 'target');

    6.2   the share transfer is executed as part of the transfer of the   ☐
whole or part of the undertakings;

    6.3   the consideration for the acquisition by the acquiring   ☐
company consists of the issue of shares in the acquiring
company to all the shareholders of target, possibly
together with the assumption or discharge of any
liabilities of target; and

    6.4   after the acquisition, the shareholders of both companies   ☐
are the same, their shares in the same relative
proportions?

7.   If the transfer does not fall into any of the aforementioned   *FA 1986, s 77*   ☐
categories, is it possible to gain exemption from stamp duty
because it is broadly a transfer where:

    7.1   shares in one company (the 'target company') are being   ☐
transferred to another company (the 'acquiring
company');

    7.2   the acquiring company is acquiring the entire share   ☐
capital of target;

    7.3   the consideration for the acquisition is the issue of shares   ☐
in the acquiring company to the shareholders of target;
and

    7.4   after the acquisition the share capital and the   ☐
shareholders of the acquiring company exactly match
that of the target company immediately before the
acquisition?

8.   If the transfer does not fall into any of the above categories have   ☐
you paid stamp duty at the rate of 50p per £100 on the
consideration subject to a minimum of £5 and rounded up to the
nearest £5?

Practical Notes

The exemptions listed under questions 5, 6 and 7 above are subject to many qualifications and professional advice should generally be sought in their application. In addition, the transfer documents will need to be submitted to the Stamp Office for them to adjudicate whether or not the transfer is exempt from stamp duty.

The consideration on which stamp duty is calculated or adjudicated may comprise, for instance:

- *cash, which may include an element to be paid at some future date dependant upon a specific requirement being met;*
- *stock or marketable securities which may be issued at the time of the transfer or at a later date which may or may not be dependant upon a specific requirement being me;*

- *non-marketable securities;*
- *periodic payments; or*
- *debt.*

In some of these cases the value of the consideration may be difficult to determine and indeed may even be subject to specific criteria. It is therefore suggested that appropriate advice should be sought, if in doubt.

For transfers involving a purchase of own shares reference should be made to Checklist 8.6 or Checklist 8.7, as appropriate.

Stamp Duty Reserve Tax ('SDRT') is charged on share transfers where there is no transfer document, as would be the case, for instance, with shares held under CREST. Duly stamping a share transfer either cancels or leads to the repayment of (depending whether the tax was paid or not) the SDRT that became payable on the date of the agreement to sell the shares. This is a specific area of stamp duty and queries in relation to this should be directed to the Worthing Stamp Office at East Block, Barrington Road, Worthing, West Sussex BN12 4XJ (Tel: 01903 508 962).

Inter vivos means a transfer between living persons or corporate bodies.

It is important to lodge forms which may need to be stamped with the Stamp Office within 30 days to ensure that no penalties are levied regardless of whether the consideration is known.

Details of your local Inland Revenue Stamp Taxes Offices can be found either by calling their helpline on 0845 603 0135 or visiting their website on www.inlandrevenue.gov.uk/so.

8.17   Class Rights

A company's share capital can be divided into shares of different classes. Each class of share may entitle the holder to different rights in respect of, for instance, voting, return of capital or distribution of surplus assets on winding up. These are known as class rights. Details of such class rights may be contained in the Articles of Association, the resolution creating that particular class of share and, in the case of older companies, in the Memorandum of Association. Members of companies often have different interests and class rights are a mechanism used to protect these interests and ensure each member can influence the company in an appropriate manner.

Holders of different classes of shares have equal voting rights unless alternative rights are imposed. For example, preference shares usually have no voting rights but it is common practice to provide for voting rights if dividend payments on such preference shares are in arrears. These rights are usually contained in the Articles of Association.

When proposing to vary the class rights of a company, the following should be considered.

Task:	Reference:	
1. Do the rights in respect of the class appear in the Articles of Association?	**Checklist 2.3**	☐
2. If the answer to question 1 above is yes, is there a mechanism for varying the class rights contained in the Articles of Association? (If so, this needs to be followed.)	**CSH 7.11**	☐
3. Do the rights appear in the Memorandum of Association but nowhere else? (If so, and the memorandum and Articles do not provide how the rights are to be varied all the members of the company need to consent to the variation.)	**Checklists 2.1, 7.6, 7.10 CSH 7.11**	☐
4. If there is a mechanism to vary the rights contained in the Articles of Association, do you need to consider passing a new resolution to allow the directors to allot shares or in connection with a reduction in capital?	*CA 1985, ss 80, 135* **Checklists 8.11**	☐
5. If there is no mechanism in the Articles of Association then either:	*CA 1985, s 125(2)* **CSH 7.11** **Checklist 7.1**	☐
5.1 the holders of three quarters in nominal value of the issued shares of that class must consent in writing to the variation; or		☐
5.2 an extraordinary resolution must be passed at a separate general meeting of the holders of that class to sanction the variation.		☐
6. If a class meeting is to be held in order to pass an extraordinary resolution has 14 days notice of the meeting been given?	*CA 1985, ss 125(6), 369*	☐
7. Has the notice been circulated to all the members of the class?	*CA 1985, ss 125(6), 370*	☐
8. Has the company notified Companies House of any variation in class rights which result in a class of shares having rights which are not stated in either the Memorandum or the Articles of Association?	*CA 1985, s 128(1)* **Checklist 5.1**	☐

9.   Do any of Forms 128(1), 128(3) or 128(4) need to be filed at   *CA 1985, s 128(4)*   ☐
     Companies House?   **Checklist 5.1**

Practical Notes

If you decide to vary the rights by obtaining the written consent of the holders of 75% in nominal value of the class, you do not need to use the usual terminology of the written resolution (CA 1985, s 381A) as here you do not need to obtain the written consent of all the members (see Checklist 7.10).

There is no definition of class rights in the Companies Act 1985 and the meaning is not entirely clear. The usual concept of a class is that it is distinct and can be differentiated from other shares due to rights of the shares in respect of, for instance, voting and dividends.

8.18   Block Listing of Shares

For securities of a company subject to the UK Listing Authority's Listing Rules to be marketable, the company may wish to be admitted to the Official List of the London Stock Exchange. Listing is carried out by the UK Listing Authority (the 'UKLA') which is run by the Financial Services Authority and was previously controlled by the London Stock Exchange.

When a company subject to the UKLA Listing Rules has issued all the shares previously admitted to the 'Official List' and proposes to make future allotment, it will need to make a further application for shares or securities to be admitted to the Official List to the London Stock Exchange and the UKLA.

If a listed company, subject to the UKLA's Listing Rules, wishes to issue small tranches of shares on a regular basis there is a procedure whereby it is exempt from producing listing particulars (LR 5.27).

The company can produce information at the time of the application which will cover the admission of a specified number of new securities for a particular period following the application. This could include issuing securities pursuant to an employees' share scheme, personal equity plan or a dividend re-investment plan, amongst others.

In these circumstances, there are two procedures which the company may follow:

- a simplified application procedure for each issue which is also known as the 'Formal Application' (LR 7.11); or
- an application for a specified number of securities which may be issued in a particular case which is known as a 'block listing' (LR 7.12).

In a **Formal Application**, the following items must be lodged with the Listing Applications section of the UKLA at least two business days prior to the consideration of the application for admission.

Task:		Reference:	✍
1.	Has a signed and dated Application for Admission of Securities to the Official List (Shares and Debt Securities) in the form provided in Schedule 3 of the Listing Rules been lodged?	**LR 7.11** **LR Schedule 3(a)**	☐
2.	Has a document in printed form detailing the number and type of securities to be admitted and the circumstances of their issue been lodged?	**LR 7.11(b)**	☐
3.	Has the appropriate fee been sent?	**LR 7.11(c)**	☐
4.	Have copies of the resolutions of the board of the issuer allotting the securities which are the subject of the application (if the market capitalisation of the company is greater than £2m) been lodged?	**LR 7.11(d)** **Checklist 6.3**	☐
5.	Has a letter (on company letterhead) to the London Stock Exchange stating that the company has not offered and will not offer the securities to which the application relates to the public in the United Kingdom been lodged?	*Financial Services and Markets Act 2000, Sch 11* **LR 7.7(b)**	☐
6.	Has a signed copy of the company's application for admission to trading been lodged?	**LR 7.11(f)**	☐

In a **Block Listing Application**, the following items must be lodged with the Listing Applications Section of the UKLA at least two business days prior to the consideration of the application for admission.

Task:		Reference:	✍

1. Has an Application for Admission of Securities to Trading in the form provided in Schedule 3 of the Listing Rules been lodged?   **LR 7.12** **LR Schedule 3A** ☐

2. Has a document in printed form detailing the number and type of securities to be admitted and the circumstances of their issue been lodged?   **LR 7.12(b)** ☐

3. Has the appropriate fee been sent?   **LR 7.12(c)** ☐

4. Has a letter (on company letterhead) to the London Stock Exchange stating that the company has not offered and will not offer the securities to which the block listing application relates to the public in the UK been lodged?   **LR 7.7(b)** ☐

5. Has a signed copy of the company's application for admission to trading been lodged?   ☐

6. Does the announcement relating to the block listing contain the following information: ☐

    6.1 the date of the application;   ☐

    6.2 the name of the company;   ☐

    6.3 the number of securities to be admitted;   ☐

    6.4 the denomination of shares; and   ☐

    6.5 the reason for the block listing application?   ☐

7. For both a block listing and a formal application: ☐

    7.1 has the UKLA contacted you to confirm approval of the application for securities to be admitted to the UK Listing Authority's Official List; and   ☐

    7.2 has a notice been issued jointly by the Financial Services Authority and the London Stock Exchange?   ☐

Practical Notes

Applications for a block listing are held every morning so it is advisable to stipulate a date when the securities are to be admitted to trading, giving at least two clear days' notice.

To check whether there is a fee for admission of the securities to the London Stock Exchange visit their website on www.londonstockexchange.com. Click on 'Services for Companies' and 'Fees Calculator' and help to calculate the admission and annual fees for securities admitted to trading is available. There is also an equity securities table available from the London Stock Exchange which helps you calculate the fee manually by establishing the market capitalisation band of the securities to be admitted. A copy of this table can be obtained from the London Stock Exchange direct on 020 7588 2355. VAT must be added to the fee calculated. There is no fee payable if the market capitalisation figure is less than £2 million.

For fees payable to FSA see www.fsa.gov.uk – fees payable FSA (Arafat Shah: 020 7676 3862).

Following a block listing application, the company must complete a block listing six monthly return and file it with a Regulatory Information Service, copied to the UK Listing Authority. Schedule 5 of the Listing Rules of the UK Listing Authority gives details of the number of securities covered by the block listing which have been allotted in the previous six months.

9 Other Useful Checklists

Contents

9.1　Post-completion Matters

It is crucial that once a company has completed a transaction, the necessary steps are taken to update the statutory registers and file appropriate documentation at Companies House. Often problems arise whereby a transaction has not been satisfactorily concluded and the company meets with queries, penalties and reminders from Companies House and other related bodies.

The following are some of the matters that should be considered after the completion of a transaction involving a company.

Task:	Reference:	✍
1.　Have the share transfer forms and agreement been stamped or adjudicated as non-chargeable from stamp duty, ensuring timely delivery of documents to the stamping office, in order to avoid penalties as penalties will be incurred if 30 day dead-line or stamping is not met?	*CA 1985 s 183(1)* **Checklist 8.16**	☐
2.　Have all appropriate forms, agreements and resolutions been filed at Companies House, dealing with, for instance:		
2.1　changes of name;	*CA 1985, ss 26(1)(2), 28(1), 29(1)-(3)* **Checklist 2.8**	☐
2.2　appointment and resignation of directors/secretaries;	*CA 1985, s 288(2)* **Checklists 1.1, 1.2, 6.1, 6.4**	☐
2.3　changes of Registered Office;	*CA 1985, s 287* **Checklist 3.7**	☐
2.4　allotments of shares; and	*CA 1985, s 88(2)* **Checklist 8.11**	☐
2.5　filing of resolutions?	*CA 1985, s 380* **Checklist 7.1**	☐
3.　Has new company stationery been prepared?	*CA 1985, s 351* **Checklist 3.10**	☐
4.　Have the following registers, if appropriate, been updated to reflect the post-completion structure:		
4.1　register of members (following stamping of documents referred to in question 1 above);	**Checklist 3.1**	☐
4.2　register of directors and secretaries?	**Checklist 3.2**	☐
4.3　register of directors interests;	**Checklist 3.3**	☐
4.4　register of loan note holders;		☐
4.5　register of charges; and	**Checklist 3.4**	☐

4.6   register of debentures?   **Checklist 3.5** ☐

5.   Are any announcements required in relation to the transaction and have these been made to comply with, for instance, the requirements of the UK Listing Authority's Listing Rules? ☐

6.   Has a letter been sent to advise employees, suppliers, customers, debtors, pensioners of change of ownership of company, new company name, registered office, etc? ☐

7.   Is a new bank mandate to reflect the change of signatories to the company's bank account required and, if so, has the resolution approving the new signatories in the bank's own standard format been prepared? ☐

8.   Has the purchaser been registered as the new owner of any intellectual property (including trademarks) and any relevant licences and assignments filed? ☐

9.   Have new employment contracts been renewed or changed for key employees? ☐

10.   Will a new pension scheme be required, or is a deed of participation required? ☐

11.   Have you arranged for the timely delivery of new share certificates?   *CA 1985, ss 36A(4), 36B(2), 185(1)* **Checklist 8.15** ☐

12.   Have the requirements relating to the maintenance of documents been satisfied?   *CA 1985, s 382* **Checklists 3.6, 3.9** ☐

13.   Have new auditors been appointed/auditors resigned, and has this been notified to Companies House?   *CA 1985, ss 392(3), 394(2)* **Checklist 4.17** ☐

Practical Notes

A copy of the bank mandate should be obtained as soon as possible in order for this to be completed and to avoid delays in the payment of staff, suppliers or otherwise.

Each transaction is different and it is not always easy or possible to anticipate the implications of the transaction. It is important to take a logical sequential approach to ensure that it is thoroughly and satisfactorily documented.

Table of Statutes

Table of Statutory Instruments

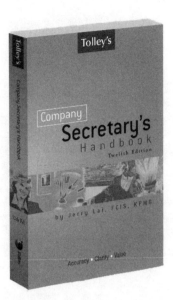

How To Order

To order, please contact LexisNexis Butterworths Tolley,
Customer Services Dept, LexisNexis Butterworths Tolley,
FREEPOST SEA 4177, Croydon, Surrey, CR9 5WZ.
Telephone: freephone 0800 ___ or fax 020 8___ 2012
email: orders.enquiries@butterworths.com

LexisNexis Butterworths Tolley